DATE DUE

2008
uncommoncrochet

uncommon

Twenty-five Projects Made from

Julie
Armstrong
Holetz

crochet
Natural Yarns and Alternative Fibers

TEN SPEED PRESS
Berkeley | Toronto

{ **DEDICATION** }

For Steve, whose love, reassurance, patience, and gourmet meals sustain me through everything.

Ten Speed Press
PO Box 7123
Berkeley, California 94707
www.tenspeed.com

Distributed in Australia by Simon and Schuster Australia, in Canada by Ten Speed Press Canada, in New Zealand by Southern Publishers Group, in South Africa by Real Books, and in the United Kingdom and Europe by Publishers Group UK.

Cover and text design by Betsy Stromberg
Photography by Angie Cao
Photo assisting by Ana Borquez
Prop styling by Peggi Jeung

Library of Congress Cataloging-in-Publication Data

Holetz, Julie Armstrong.
  Uncommon crochet : twenty-five projects made from natural yarns and alternative fibers / Julie Armstrong Holetz.
     p. cm.
  Summary: "A full-color collection of twenty-five innovative patterns for crocheted bags, vases, containers, totes, baskets, and more, using unconventional yarns and fibers"—Provided by publisher.
  Includes index.
  ISBN-13: 978-1-58008-858-9 (alk. paper)
  ISBN-10: 1-58008-858-9 (alk. paper)
  1. Crocheting. 2. Crocheting—Patterns. I. Title.
TT825.H546 2008
746.43'4041—dc22

                              2007040982

Printed in Thailand
First printing, 2008

1 2 3 4 5 6 7 8 9 10 — 12 11 10 09 08

CONTENTS

ACKNOWLEDGMENTS

To my editor, Julie Bennett, thank you for your patience, dedication, and attention to detail and for pushing me to go beyond my technical skills to allow my voice to come through. To Angie Cao and Ana Borquez, for a beautiful interpretation of style through the eye of a camera; to Peggi Jeung, "it's called stylin'!"; to Betsy Stromberg, for a brilliant design aesthetic and youthful hands; to Amy Swenson, for keen tech editing; to Curtis Lowe, for his invaluable support; to Gertrude and Robert Allen, for the use of their beautiful home; and to all of the fantastic folks rockin' it at Ten Speed Press.

Many trays of sashimi go to my good friend Gonzalo Ferreyra. If he had not brought the two Julies together, it is possible that this book never would have been written.

Special thanks go to my friends in the business who have supported me in so many ways: To Kim Werker, for taking a chance at the very beginning. We predicted adventures in crochet, but who knew they would really happen? To Shannon Okey, who is always pushing the boundaries of the business and providing the inspiration and motivation to just go for it (we are the Fiber League!). To Chloe,

for your crabby friendship, cartoons, and stories that kept me going in the wee hours of the night. To Josi, Laura, Lisa, Katie, Anne, and Bean, for your support, inspiration, and friendship as creators, businesswomen, and mothers.

Many thanks to Mindy Oliver for her design input; to Jenna for her editing input at the very beginning; to Scott for his advice, food, and babysitting time; to Sue, Rachel, Amy, JoAnn, Angie, Suzanne, and Marti for entertaining the kids so their summer wasn't a complete loss; to Beth who has always been there with her sage advice and confidence in my abilities; to Gordon for being one of my biggest fans; and to my in-laws, who are so encouraging and enthusiastic about all of my projects.

I'd like to thank my family, who must be credited with my creative genes: my dad, the visual artist behind the lens; my mom, for whom crafting must involve power tools; and my grandma, who always kept my summers busy with paints, hooks, and needles.

Finally, my eternal love and appreciation go to Ally and Thad, who selflessly banded together to fill their days with something to do while I furiously crocheted.

WHAT'S UNCOMMON ABOUT CROCHET?

The '70s defined my childhood: flower power, bell bottoms, feathered hair, and big glasses. My mother was enthusiastic about contemporary American crafts of the time and my grandmother, a more traditional artist, sewed her own clothes and embroidered samplers for the kitchen wall. Between the two of them, I kept busy learning and practicing arts and crafts like macramé, sewing, embroidery, rug hooking, and, of course, crochet. As for fiber, anything could and would be used. At that time, traditional wools and acrylics were abundant in bold, incongruous colors, but the needlework artists of the '70s went way beyond the traditional yarns and threads to express their individuality with fiber-like materials, including twine, hemp, raffia, wire, and leather cord.

Becoming a mother of my own little family reminded me of my crafty roots, so once again I turned to crochet. My first project was a dense, crunchy, acrylic baby blanket that saw only four inches of life before it was retired to what would soon become an overflowing, unfinished-projects bin. I desperately searched for contemporary patterns that would inspire me and when I couldn't find them, I turned to knitting. My first completed knit project was an adorable baby sweater pattern I found in a friend's old copy of *Mon Tricot*, a popular needlework magazine from the '70s and '80s. Six weeks later, and fueled with the satisfaction of victory over knitting, I decided that I could have crocheted a similar sweater in a fraction of the time. So, I set about designing my first crochet project.

As I began to master basic crochet and design techniques, I realized I was no longer limited to crocheting long, flat squares and tubes. And I didn't need to find the perfect pattern to inspire me—I could create it myself. At first I remained true to the selections of fiber found in the yarn section of my local craft store, but eventually I wanted more. Impressed by crochet's seemingly endless design flexibility, I wanted to bend and sculpt more unusual fiber in a way that would highlight or even contradict its nature: imitating woven baskets or ceramic objects with crocheted plant fibers.

As my options for crochet design and materials expanded, so did my collection of stuff. Spools of leather cord bought off the Internet for a steal . . . overflowing tubs of multicolored fabric swatches . . . twisted loops of copper wire, floral wire, and lots of other types of wire . . . I yearned for a way to organize my stash of goods. And so while I'd like to say that the projects in *Uncommon Crochet* were inspired by seventeenth-century French textiles or the Art Nouveau paintings of Gustav Klimt, the truth is I just needed to get the stuff off my bedroom floor.

I started by designing smaller bags and baskets so I could experiment with new fibers and techniques. Then I revisited traditional fibers with a new purpose. Instead of crocheting a project, I wanted to create crocheted *fabric* that could be cut and sewn like other textiles. I discovered that wool could be felted into a fabric that defies its natural inclination to stretch, and cute felted bowls quickly filled with extra buttons, stray coins, and a surprisingly large collection of safety pins. And when the pins got out of hand, I made pincushions! No container was safe: totes, baskets, vases . . . they can all be crocheted, and I'll show you how.

In "Building Your Stash," I'll tell you about the huge variety of tools, fibers, and other materials available to the modern crocheter. While many of the fibers used here can be found in traditional yarn shops, some have to be tracked down at the local home improvement store, on the Internet, or possibly in a forgotten corner of your garage. But don't worry, I'll tell you where and how to buy, scrounge, or recycle everything you need.

In "Mastering the Basics," I walk beginners through the standard crochet stitches step by step, teaching you everything you need to know to get started, from how to read the pattern to how to fasten off the fiber when you're done. In "Trying New Techniques," I show you how to work the techniques found in this book (well, actually, in any book) that go beyond the basics. Once you've got the stitches down, I'll touch on alternative ways of using them to create unexpected shapes and textures.

The projects in *Uncommon Crochet* appear in three chapters dedicated to different crafting approaches: "Create," "Design," and "Experiment." The patterns in "Create" feature both traditional and nontraditional materials. When you crochet with uncommon fibers, complicated stitch patterns can get lost. These projects keep it simple, while allowing you to play with construction techniques.

In "Design," I take things one step further, outlining the basic principles you need to know before you design your own project. Whether you're a dedicated pattern follower or someone who likes to make it up as you go,

I provide inspiration and techniques to encourage your creative spirit. After you master a few of the projects in this section, you will have the tools and know-how to design your own projects.

In "Experiment," things get fun and funky with ideas for creating and embellishing your own or other projects. Wire, felted beads, even crocheted sushi—this section encourages you to use everything you know to make every project a reflection of your personal style. There are some great gift ideas here, or just make a few of these projects because they look like fun; either way, this section gives you permission to step way outside the box.

While crochet itself isn't necessarily uncommon, what you choose to make and work with can be. My purpose in writing *Uncommon Crochet* was to motivate others to play with structure, fiber, and design, to abandon the norm, to ask questions, and to simply create with what you know or what you want to discover.

{ 1 }

BUILDING YOUR STASH

You know what truly rocks about crochet? All you really need to get started is some sort of fiber and a crochet hook. These two things are all you need for most projects, but since we all like acquiring cool stuff, of course there are a few additional items you'll want to pick up to make your crochetin' life a bit easier. In this chapter, I explore a variety of fibers you can crochet with along with the necessary (and sometimes not so necessary, but nice to have) tools you need to finish up your project. Although I only discuss fibers used in this book, there are plenty of other materials you can experiment with if the mood strikes, including nylon twine, plastic grocery bags, gardening tape, video tape, plastic lace, string licorice—even cooked spaghetti. The possibilities are endless, so let's get started.

FIBERS

Your personal collection of yarn or fibers that sit around in a pile waiting to be stitched up is called a *stash*. Whether you bought a skein of yarn for a specific project or found a spool of bright blue wire at a yard sale, it's easy to suddenly find yourself with an overflowing stash bin.

Today, the options for fiber are countless and limited only by your imagination. Of course, you can buy traditional yarn and thread in yarn stores, but there is lots of life beyond the craft shop. Think about crocheted jute doormats and plant hangers that were all the rage in the '70s and hit your local hardware store to sample thick cord and twine. If colorful wire is more your thing, jewelry supply stores offer an abundance of materials ready for the hook. If it can be sewn, glued, or somehow made into one continuous strand, you can probably crochet with it. Flip through the projects in this book and I'm sure you'll find something that piques your interest.

Following is a list of the fibers used in *Uncommon Crochet*, whether they are traditional, uncommon, or downright unexpected. I tell you where and how to buy each fiber, and I've listed projects that use each type of fiber in case you are trying to figure out what to do with that spool of hot pink raffia you bought last summer.

Animal Fibers

These are traditional yarns in which at least 50 percent of the fiber content comes from an animal (like sheep's wool or alpaca). In their natural state, animal fibers typically work up into a soft, stretchy fabric; however, with a little hot water and soap they will become a sturdy, felted fabric that can be easily cut, sewn, or formed into three-dimensional projects like bags, flowers, and bowls. Because animal fibers have more stretch than plant fibers, projects that require strength or need to maintain their structure, like baskets and bowls, must be combined with inelastic materials like cotton thread, lined with fabric, or felted (see page 42). Most animal fibers are available at yarn stores and craft shops. Projects made with animal fibers include: The Tube Bag (page 57), Vintage Satchel (page 73), The Perfect Bin (page 93), and Martini Bag (page 153).

Cotton

Cotton is a natural plant fiber that yields beautiful stitch definition. It is also soft, strong, durable, and inelastic, which means it's highly adaptable and perfect for a variety of projects: sculpted vases, stiff containers, even loose and lacy bags. Cotton takes on a supporting role when carried along with fibers that need added strength or rigidity (like animal fibers above). Cotton is available in different thicknesses, from threads to cords, and can be found in craft, fabric, and yarn shops. Projects made with cotton include: Vintage Satchel (page 73), Sake Set (page 131), and Sushi (page 135).

Fabric Remnants

I *love* strolling through fabric stores, letting the bold colors and patterns spark my creativity while I run my hands across the funky new textures. Although I enjoy cruising wall after wall of fabric, I usually end up buying from remnant or clearance bins, where you can find small pieces of fabric at great prices. If you build a stash of remnants, you'll always have some material ready for a last-minute project.

Choose your fabric based on its intended use, whether it's for lining a bag or creating a long strand of material to crochet with. Although most bag linings aren't seen from the outside, I honestly think that a lining can make or break a piece—even if I'm the only one who knows it's there! Since a lining bears the weight of the bag's contents, choose a sturdy and easy-to-use fabric like cotton or a cotton-blend that contains at least 50 percent cotton. Silky fabrics are more difficult to sew, but they make a gorgeous swishy and loose lining.

Crocheting with fabric is a great way to use scraps or recycle old clothes and linens. Consider the weight, fiber content, and width of the fabric before you start crocheting. Heavy fabrics like denim will be difficult to work with and require a larger hook than light- to medium-weight cotton blends. Fabrics that have some stretch, like polyester, are easy to work with, but keep in mind that your final crocheted piece will also have some stretch. Cotton, linen, and silk tend to be quite durable. Avoid thick fabrics or fabrics that fall apart when cut. The width of the strips you use determines the size of the hook you'll need: the wider the strip, the larger the hook. Before you buy new fabric off the bolt, rummage through your closet for unwanted clothes or linens, or visit a local thrift store for something that's new to you. Projects made with fabric

remnants include: Vintage Satchel (page 73), Patchwork Handbag (page 77), Yo-Yo Basket Bag (page 101), Strappy Clutch (page 107), and Geometric Pincushions (page 119).

Hemp

Commonly used for making jewelry, macramé pieces, and many other crafts, hemp is a perfect fiber for crochet projects that require strength and firmness. Usually found in craft or jewelry stores, hemp comes in a variety of sizes and colors, and tends to be labeled by thickness (in millimeters) or the amount of weight a strand can hold before it breaks (in pounds). For ease of use and flexibility, 1.0 mm or 20 lb hemp twine is best for most crochet projects (and those found in this book). Hemp works well for structured, three-dimensional projects like vases and boxes, but it can also be softened with a simple wet block (see page 45) to create soft yet sturdy fabric for bags. Projects made with hemp include: Patchwork Handbag (page 77), Petite Fleur Vases (page 145), and Lace Vases (page 149).

Jute

Jute is a strong plant fiber that's ideal for bags, containers, or any project requiring a stiff fabric. When you crochet with jute, you end up with an interesting fibrous texture and beautiful stitch definition. Natural jute, which comes in neutral shades, is readily available in a variety of thicknesses (measured in millimeters or plies) at hardware, gardening, or craft stores. You can also find an assortment of colored jute twine at gift or packaging supply stores. Use 2 to 3 mm (or 2 to 3 ply) twine for the projects in this book. Projects made with jute include: Jute Filet Bag (page 69), The Perfect Bin (page 93), Geometric Pincushions (page 119), Jute Vase (page 127), and Lace Vases (page 149).

Leather Cord

Leather is truly a luxury to crochet with because it retains its form and stitch definition beautifully. You can buy leather cord in 25- and 100-yard (23 and 91 m) hanks or spools or by the yard, and it comes in several colors and thicknesses (measured in millimeters). Right off the spool, leather tends to be pretty stiff, so wind it up into a ball before you attempt to crochet with it to soften up the cord. (Or if you're lucky enough to live in a warm climate, set up your chair in a sunny spot and the leather will soften with the sun's warmth as you work.) Look for 1.0 and 2.0 mm spools to make the sculpted crochet projects in this book. Although leather cord is easily found in the jewelry department of your local craft store, it may be less expensive to buy through online jewelry supply and auction sites, where you may get a discount for buying in bulk. Projects made with leather include: Red's Goodie Basket (page 95), Leather Grannies (page 99), and Petite Fleur Vases (page 145).

Raffia

Natural raffia, made from strands of palm fiber, is commonly used as packaging string. It can be tricky to crochet with, as it tends to be fibrous and lacks a uniform texture. Synthetic raffia, which creates a crisp and crunchy fabric when crocheted, is similar to crocheting with 1/4- to 1/2-inch (0.5 to 1 cm) ribbon. After blocking (see page 47) raffia, the strands will loosen up and the stitches will relax, softening the fabric and creating a more fluid drape. Natural raffia is usually packaged in bags and synthetic raffia is available in a wide range of colors on spools; both can be found at craft, floral, or packaging supply stores. Projects made with raffia include: Random Stripe Tote (page 111).

Sisal

Like jute, sisal is a thick plant fiber with lots of texture. Strong and durable, sisal is suitable for crocheted planter boxes, baskets, floor mats, and bags. Because of its thickness, working with sisal requires a large crochet hook—6.5 to 10 mm—and a bit of arm strength. If your sisal fabric curls along the edges as you work, try wet blocking it (see page 45) to relax the fiber, smoothing out the stitches and flattening the edges. Sisal can be found in home improvement, gardening, and some craft stores. Projects made with sisal include: Yo-Yo Basket Bag (page 101) and Pacific Coast Basket (page 115).

String

Usually made with 100 percent cotton, linen, or a cotton-acrylic blend, household or kitchen string is a strong, inelastic material that shows beautiful stitch definition. Because of its strength and durability, it's well suited for bags and structured containers. Buy string at hardware, grocery, packaging, or kitchen supply stores. Projects made with string include: Strappy Clutch (page 107), Sake Set (page 131), Corde Market Bag (page 139), Petite Fleur Vases (page 145), and Lace Vases (page 149).

Recycled Materials

Using recycled sweaters, bags, and belts for your crochet projects not only makes you an environmentally conscious crafter, but it also gives you a bounty of unique project supplies. When searching for items to recycle, consider the following: What is the fiber content of the material (will it felt, will it unravel when you cut it)? How much effort will it take to deconstruct the item (can you just cut it into pieces, do you have to take it apart stitch by stitch)? Is the deconstruction effort worth your time?

Old handbags have a lot to offer. Before you buy, take a moment to consider how much of it is recyclable. Look for straps, closures, drawstring cords, split rings, zippers, and reusable fabric. Straps on swivel hooks are super easy to use; just unhook and you're done. A strap that is connected to the bag with a ring can be easily detached by cutting through the connecting tab. A bag with straps that have been sewn on will require a seam ripper and a lot more time. Take time to inspect the item carefully to make sure you're getting what you're looking for. Is the leather real or fake? Are the straps and closures sewn or glued to the bag? Do the zippers and closures work? By understanding how the item was originally created, you'll have an easier time taking it apart and reusing the pieces.

Old belts have great potential for becoming bag straps. Novelty and web belts with rings can be attached to a bag with a simple fabric or crocheted tab that is looped through the ring, then sewn to the sides of the bag. Leather belts make good, strong straps, but they may need to be cut, sewn, or otherwise altered before use.

The easiest way to reuse a sweater or scarf is to felt it (see page 42), then cut it up and use the pieces for quilts, bags, scarves, and so on. To determine whether a sweater can be felted, check the label for fiber content and care instructions. Sweaters made with 85 to 100 percent animal fibers can be felted, but keep in mind that many sweaters are treated so they can be machine washed. If the care instructions say something like "hand wash in cold water" or "do not wring," the sweater will probably felt. Machine washable items won't felt.

A more complicated way to recycle a sweater is to take it apart at the seams. You can either reuse the shaped pieces (sleeves, back, neck) to make bags and accessories or embellish other projects, or unravel the yarn entirely to add to your stash. If the seams have been serged, which is a machine-made overcast stitch usually worked on raw edges to keep them from fraying, move on to the next sweater. Serged seams tell you that the edges have been cut and the yarn won't unravel in one continuous strand. Stretch the seam to determine how it was created. If the seam stitches are easily discernible, the stitches can be quickly snipped to separate the pieces. Once a section has been detached, simply snip the last stitch and begin to unravel. Also check the item's fiber content. Acrylic yarns might not be worth your time, and fuzzy yarns are likely to get tangled when you try to unravel them. Finally, look at the size of the stitches. If they are itty bitty, the yarn is pretty thin. Do you really want to reuse super thin yarn with a tiny little hook?

Whether it's being "green," cheap, or resourceful, recycling will open up a lot of creative opportunities. Projects made with recycled materials include: Hong Kong Bag (page 59), The Perfect Bin (page 93), Strappy Clutch (page 107), and Random Stripe Tote (page 111). Recycling and reusing never looked so good!

Wire

Readily available in craft, bead, and home improvement or electronics stores, wire comes in a variety of metals, colors, and sizes. Wire is measured in terms of *gauge*, which describes the diameter of the wire. The higher the gauge number, the thinner and more flexible the wire will be. I like to crochet with wire that measures 24 to 30 gauge for bigger projects and 28 to 30 gauge for delicate projects like jewelry or small containers. In my opinion, wire that has a gauge lower than 24 or a gauge higher than 30 is too difficult to manipulate. Whatever gauge you choose, be sure to handle the wire carefully because it can break easily. The wire's thickness and the desired tightness of the stitches will determine the appropriate hook size for your project. If you use a thick wire or want a loose, lacy look, try using a hook in the 6.5 mm to 9 mm range. If you use a thin wire or want a tight, solid-looking fabric, try using a hook in the 1.8 mm to 4.0 mm range.

If you've never worked with wire, resist the urge to use silver tone craft wire for your first project. Although it's cheap and easy to find, craft wire is more difficult to work with than other wires. It will eat up your hooks and leave you with calluses on your fingers. A gentle, beginner-friendly wire is copper. It's soft and pliable, comes in a variety of colors, and tends to be less expensive than other fine metal wires. Projects made with wire include: Jute Vase (page 127), Wire Flower (page 143), and Petite Fleur Vases (page 145).

TOOLS

Once you've decided what type of fiber you're going to use, the next step is to choose a hook and gather together the rest of the tools that make design and construction simple.

Ball Winder

A ball winder is great for winding hanks of yarn and thin-to medium-weight fibers into a nifty little center-pull ball.

Chalk

Chalk is used for marking and tracing cut lines. You can find tailor's chalk in the sewing supplies section of any fabric store, but I usually borrow standard blackboard chalk from my kids and it works just as well. If you don't feel like buying chalk, you can mark and trace on fabric with a sliver of soap.

Clear Ruler

A clear, rigid ruler is one way to assess your gauge (see Gauge Tool below). Lay the ruler on top of your fabric, and when you press down, you'll be able to see your stitches clearly through the ruler. Another benefit of a rigid ruler: it can't be stretched out of shape (by a little person who shall remain nameless) like measuring tape.

Crochet Hook Case

Once you've amassed a collection of hooks, you may find that it's difficult to keep track of the different sizes. My first case was a small zippered bag. After a while, I had too many hooks for the bag, and every time I wanted a specific one I had to dump all of them out, find the right one, then put all of them back. My husband must have heard me grumbling because he snuck off and found an artist who uses remnant vintage fabrics and buttons to create customized hook cases. Now I have a roll-up case with pockets to slide the hooks into. Because crochet hooks are typically between five and seven inches in length, you can fit a dozen or so hooks in the case, roll it up, and throw it in your purse.

Hook rolls and cases are available at most retail and online craft stores. Some specialty Internet retailers like Crippenworks (see Resources), will customize cases to your specifications and add pockets for small scissors, a measuring tape, and yarn needles. You could also make your own crochet case or roll by felting crocheted or recycled wool fabrics so the hooks don't poke through the fabric.

Gauge Tool

When measuring a crocheted piece of fabric, the gauge refers to the number of stitches and rows within a certain space. A gauge tool has a ruler that allows you to measure your stitches and confirm that you are using the proper fiber and hook size for the project you're making. You might also find little holes on a gauge tool that let you measure the size of your hooks. (See page 34 for more information about gauge and why it is so important.)

Hooks

The variety of hooks available makes my head spin. Standard crochet hooks are made from plastic, aluminum, wood, ivory, bone, bamboo, steel, casein, and bailene. Specialty hooks are lovingly handmade from mother-of-pearl, glass, or even with an LED so you can work in the dark. You can also buy hooks for very specific uses, like Tunisian, Afghan, and double-ended hooks, but we aren't using them here, so I won't go into detail about them.

Although I love to collect unique and handcrafted hooks, my favorite hooks to work with are polished aluminum. They are strong enough to work with tough fibers like leather cord and jute without bending. For softer fibers like wool and cotton, the smooth polished hooks will make your stitches fly. Plastic and bamboo hooks have the advantage of being lightweight, but they tend to bend when working with tight stitches or tough fibers and occasionally snag on fuzzier fibers like wool.

I find it confusing and slightly annoying that hook sizes are classified in so many different ways. Most hooks are designated with a letter, a number, and a metric measurement expressed in millimeters (mm). Usually the smaller the number or letter, the thinner the hook—except if we're talking about steel crochet hooks, and then it's reversed: the smaller the number, the thicker the hook. Confusing, right? The metric measurement represents the actual diameter of the shaft, which is the part of the hook you grab with your hand. This is really the only size designation that makes any sense to me. So in this book, I refer to the metric measurement when I call for a specific hook. This measurement is universal. If you happen to have a hook that doesn't show the metric measurement or if you want to double-check the size, use a gauge tool (see above) to verify the size.

Hooks are relatively inexpensive, so if you're like me, you'll probably find yourself with a surprisingly large cache of hooks after a while. I often stash a hook or two in my purse, my car, my workout bag, my husband's car, and lots of other places. That way, there's always a hook around when the inspiration hits me.

Hook Sizes and Conversions		
2.25 mm	B	1
2.75 mm	C	2
3.25 mm	D	3
3.50 mm	E	4
3.75 mm	F	5
4.00 mm	G	6
4.50 mm	G	7
5.00 mm	H	8
5.50 mm	I	9
6.00 mm	J	10
6.50 mm	K	10½
8.00 mm	L	11
9.00 mm	M or N	13
10.00 mm	N or P	15
15.00 mm	P or Q	—
16.00 mm	Q	—
19.00 mm	S	—

Iron

Use an iron with a steam setting for steam blocking crocheted fabric, pressing hems, and ironing fabrics.

Measuring Tape

A measuring tape is handy for measuring the dimensions of curved and flat surfaces, and it's a good backup for measuring gauge if you don't have a ruler or gauge tool on hand.

Needles

Standard sewing needles, called sharps, are used for hand stitching with thread, sewing woven fabrics together, and adding fabric linings to projects.

Embroidery needles are similar to standard sewing needles except they have an elongated eye to accommodate embroidery floss and threads.

Yarn needles, also called tapestry needles, are bigger and thicker than standard sewing needles and have a large eye for use with yarns and other thick fibers. Use yarn needles to weave in the tail ends of fibers and join pieces together.

It's nice to have needles of differing sizes on hand because you never know what type of needle you'll need. Small portable needle cases hold needles of all sizes, or you can make a Geometric Pincushion (page 119) to keep your needles safe in one place.

Pins

Use straight pins or safety pins to hold crocheted pieces in place while you sew them together. Rust-proof straight pins are great for holding fabric in place while blocking.

Project Bag

A project bag or basket is a tidy way to keep your WIP (works in progress) organized. But, hey! Why buy one? Make Red's Goodie Basket (page 95) or use the tips, techniques, and projects in this book to design your own.

Rotary Cutter and Cutting Mat

If you expect to be cutting a lot of fabric, you may want to invest in a rotary cutter and cutting mat. The rotary cutter looks a little bit like a pizza cutter and it's used to cut fabrics cleanly. The blade is round and very sharp, which makes the task of cutting fabrics quick and neat. The cutting mat has gridlike rule lines along both edges to help you line up fabric edges and cut straight lines.

Seam Ripper

A seam ripper is a handy little tool used for removing unwanted seams or stitches. The working end of the ripper looks like a fork with two points. The longer side narrows into a sharp point, while the shorter side has a little ball on the end to protect the fabric. Between the two points is a sharp, curved blade. To use a seam ripper, slide the pointed end under the thread to be removed and keep sliding it forward until the blade cuts the thread. Seam rippers, which are inexpensive and found in fabric shops, are great for deconstructing recycled items like bag straps and closures.

Stitch Markers

Stitch markers are some of the handiest little tools in your crochet arsenal. They do the work of remembering where to place stitches so you don't have to. If you find that you drop or add stitches at the edge of a project, just place a marker in the first and last stitches so you know where to stop and where to start on each row. When working in a spiral round, place a stitch marker in the first stitch of each round to help you keep track of how many rounds you've made. You can also use markers to help you remember where another piece of fabric will be joined later on.

You don't have to buy stitch markers; you can use a scrap of contrasting colored yarn, a safety pin, or an earring. You can also make your own markers with beads and memory wire or necklace closures like S-hooks and lobster claws. If you do buy stitch markers, be sure to purchase *removable* markers, and not the closed O-rings that knitters use. You won't be able to remove them, so they don't work for crochet.

Thread

Sewing thread is used for sewing woven fabrics together and sewing linings into crocheted projects. If the thread won't show, choose any thread color you like. If the seam line will show, be sure to use a thread color that coordinates with your fabric or it'll just look sloppy. Thread is easy to find in any fabric store, but also check out thrift stores for bags of thread in all colors and sizes for only a couple of bucks. This is a great way to get your thread stash started.

Embroidery thread is great to have on hand for embellishing your projects with embroidery stitches or appliqués. Embroidery floss and Perle cotton, two common varieties of embroidery thread, are composed of several strands of thread. It is thicker than sewing thread, but can be separated into individual strands for fine stitch work. Floss is relatively inexpensive and comes in a wide range of colors.

✳   ✳   ✳   ✳   ✳

Whether you have nothing more than a hook and a ball of string, or a stockpile of the latest tools and fibers, now you're ready to get started. In the next chapter, I explain the basic stitches to get you started. So, ready your hook and let's get stitching.

{ 2 }

MASTERING THE BASICS

This chapter is about the basics: how to hold the hook, how to form the stitches, and how to fasten off the fiber at the end. I'll show you the most common way of working each stitch, and explore alternative methods that go beyond the basics so you can be comfortable reading patterns found in this book and others. For beginner crocheters and those who need to review the basics, this is the best place to start. Those of you who have been around the hook a few times may want to give this section a quick review to see if there's anything new (like foundation stitch rows on page 20) and to get up to speed on how I work my patterns. Like most needle arts, crochet has its own language and a whole set of abbreviations. I include the standard abbreviation for each stitch so you get used to seeing it, and a list of commonly used abbreviations also appears at the end of the book for easy reference.

GETTING STARTED

You have your hook, you have your fiber, so now what?

Wind It Up

Sometimes it's necessary to wind your fiber into a ball before you start working a project. Yarns that come in large loops get tangled if you try working directly from them, and if you make your own fiber (for instance, with strips of fabric), it's smart to wind it up before you start crocheting.

Begin by wrapping one end of the fiber around two or three of your fingers ten times. Pull the loop off your fingers, rotate the loop a quarter turn, then continue to wrap the fiber around the loop ten more times. Keep rotating and wrapping the fiber about ten times in each direction and a neat little ball will take shape.

Get a Grip: Holding Your Hook

There is more than one way to hold the hook, but I've found that the knife hold works best for getting the leverage you need to manipulate thick fibers like some of those found in this book. Grasp the hook from the top and hold it as you would a steak knife with the hook end facing down. Once you've made a few stitches, take a look at one of them from the top of the row. Each stitch

consists of two strands that form a teardrop shape (see photo below left). When you insert the hook from front to back (see arrow), slide the hook under both strands of the teardrop.

All of the instructions in this book assume that you are using your right hand to hold the hook and your left hand to control the working fiber coming off the spool or ball, working in a right to left direction. Lefties hold the hook in the left hand, controlling the yarn with the right hand and working in a left to right direction. Because the stitches in this book are explained for right-handers, left-handers will need to reverse the instructions as though working in mirror image. For comprehensive stitch and video guides aimed at left-handed crocheters, visit Art of Crochet at www.artofcrochet.com or Crochet Guild of America at www.crochet.org, or check out Donna Kooler's *Encyclopedia of Crochet* (Leisure Arts, 2002).

Tail End versus Working End

When working with any continuous length of fiber, there is always a tail end and a working end. The tail end is usually hanging out at the beginning or end of the fabric or anywhere where you have made a cut or added a new strand. The working end is the strand that is actually coming off the spool or ball of fiber.

Holding the Yarn

Ask a group of crocheters how they hold their yarn and you're likely to get a few different answers. Some people wrap the yarn once or twice around the index finger and others weave it through the fingers. How you hold the yarn determines how much tension is applied to the yarn as it flows to the fabric. The whole point is to allow the yarn to flow freely while maintaining an even tension, so experiment with your method of holding the yarn to figure out what works best for you.

To try my method, begin by holding the hook with your right hand and placing a slip knot (see page 18) on the hook with six inches of fiber hanging down to create the tail end (see page 15). With your left palm

> **TIP:** I once had a student who kept reversing the yarn over, bringing the yarn under the hook instead of over the top. I showed her the proper way to work the yarn over, then asked her how she would explain it to me if I were her student. She came up with an explanation that made sense to her and never had a problem with it again. So, if you find that you just can't get the hang of a particular movement or stitch when following someone else's instructions, try coming up with an explanation that makes sense to you and you should be good to go.

facing down, bring the working end of the fiber up between your pinkie and ring fingers, over your ring finger, under your middle finger, and over your index finger, then pinch the tail end between the thumb and middle finger of your left hand to anchor the fabric as you stitch.

Yarn Over (yo)

The term *yarn over* means to wrap the working fiber over the top of the hook from back to front. You can do this by wrapping the fiber up and over the hook from back to front with the left hand or by sweeping the hook itself under the working fiber from front to back with the right hand.

Right Side (RS) and Wrong Side (WS)

The right side of the fabric is the front of the fabric and the wrong side of the fabric is the back. The right side is easy to distinguish when you are working a project in the round in one direction because it's the side that is facing you as you work. When working back and forth in rows, you may not be able to tell the difference between one side and the other, but if it is important the pattern will instruct you to mark the right side so you can keep track. A safety pin or scrap of yarn attached to the front of the stitch is a simple way of marking the side you need to keep track of. If the pattern does not specify which is the right side, check the beginning tail. If the tail left at the beginning of the foundation chain is hanging down from the bottom left corner of the fabric, the right side is facing you.

Turning the Work

At the end of a row or round, you will usually be instructed to turn the work. Unless otherwise directed, take the piece of fabric you're working on and flip it over as though you were turning the page of a book.

Work Even

Work in the established pattern across the row or round without any increases or decreases.

Work in Established Pattern

Continue to work the same pattern of stitches and rows that were described in the Stitch Guide or have been established in the preceding rows.

Frog

To frog means to rip back or unravel the work you've done. Whether you've made a mistake or you just hate

the way the stitches are turning out, you may need to unravel the yarn at some point. Begin by removing the hook from the loop, then carefully pull the working end of the yarn to unravel each stitch until you reach the point where you would like to begin again.

Fasten Off

You fasten off when you've finished crocheting a piece. To fasten off, complete the last stitch, leaving one loop on the hook. Cut the yarn, leaving a tail of four to six inches, and pull the tail end through the loop on the hook. Grab the tail and pull firmly to cinch the knot against the fabric.

THE STITCHES

Following are descriptions of the basic stitches. You can combine and adapt any number of them to form simple or complex stitch patterns. Check out *300 Crochet Stitches (The Harmony Guides Volume 6)* and *220 More Crochet Stitches (The Harmony Guides Volume 7)* by Collins & Brown (1999). These two books are essential resources for any crochet library. Each volume features patterns and techniques, including basic stitches, lace patterns, textured patterns, motifs, and edgings.

Slip Knot

Most projects will start with a slip knot. The slip knot is the very first loop you insert the hook into and it anchors the foundation row of stitches.

To make a slip knot:

1. Leaving a tail about 6 inches (15 cm) long, wrap the fiber around the first two fingers. Cross the working end over the tail end to form a loop (see photo A on page 19).

2. Use a hook to reach through the loop, catch the working end, and draw a new loop up through the center (see photo B on page 19).

3. Keeping the hook in the new loop, remove the fiber from your fingers and gently tug the tail and working ends to tighten the knot, closing it around the hook (see photo C on page 19). The slip knot should be snug but loose enough to slide easily along the hook.

Foundation Row

Once you've made the slip knot, your next step in any project is to make a foundation row of stitches. You will build on the foundation row with additional rows of stitches to form your fabric. The most common stitch used to make the foundation row is the chain stitch (see photo on page 19), but you can also create foundation rows that combine the chain stitch and a basic stitch—like the single or double crochet stitch—at the same time. But more about that later.

Chain Stitch (ch)

The chain stitch (see bottom right photo on page 19) is a slim, compact stitch that makes the foundation row edge taut and resistant to stretching. It is important to make each chain stitch loose so the foundation edge is even with the fatter stitches you will use in subsequent rows. Keep in mind that the loop on the hook does not count as a chain stitch.

To make a row of chain stitches:

1. Put a slip knot on the hook.

2. Yarn over.

3. Catch the fiber with the hook and pull it through the loop on the hook. You have made one chain.

4. Repeat steps 2 and 3 to make the number of chains called for in your pattern. The loop on the hook and the beginning slip knot do not count as chain stitches.

TIP: If you have trouble getting the hook through the stitch, try loosening the amount of tension in your left hand, keep the chain stitches loose, and point the grooved end of the hook toward the inside V of the stitch as it slides through.

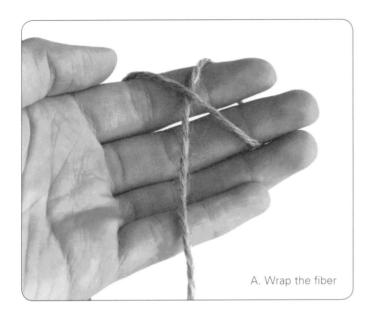

A. Wrap the fiber

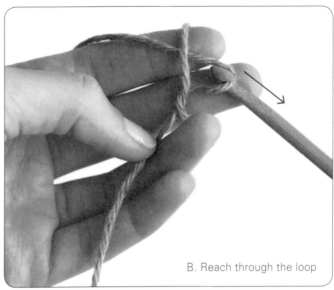

B. Reach through the loop

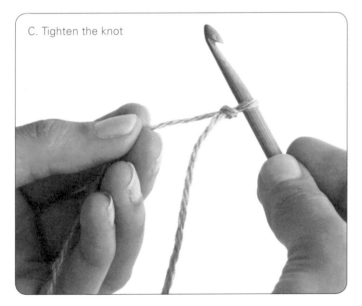

C. Tighten the knot

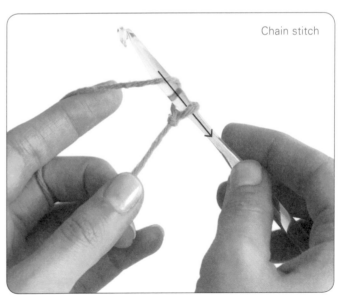

Chain stitch

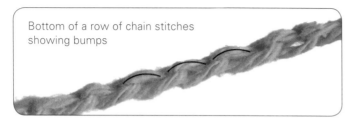

Bottom of a row of chain stitches showing bumps

Once you've completed several chain stitches, take a close look at one of the stitches. You will see that two strands form a teardrop shape on one side (see photo on page 15) and a third strand forms a ridge or bump behind it (see photo above). Unless otherwise instructed, you will insert the hook under both loops of the teardrop shape, leaving the bump under the hook. Occasionally, you may be instructed to insert your hook through the bump on the back. When working through the bump of the chain stitch, the remaining loops of the stitch are left open so they resemble the last row of your project, giving it a balanced appearance.

Turning Chain (tch)

Every time you begin a new row you need to make a number of chain stitches to get the hook up to the height of the new row. These chains keep the edges of the fabric neat. The number of chain stitches you make varies by stitch and is called a turning chain. While the turning chains listed below may be the standard, they are not the law. Turning chains give the edge of your fabric a straight edge; however, depending on your tension, the standard

turning chain may create an undesirable gap in the fabric. If you use one less turning chain for the stitch and work the first stitch into the first stitch of the previous row you can fill the gap.

For most stitches the turning chain will replace the first stitch of the row, which means you should skip the first stitch from the previous row and begin in the next stitch. The only exception is for single crochet stitches. In most patterns, the turning chain for the single crochet does not act as the first stitch, so the first single crochet is worked into the loops of the first stitch from the previous row.

Stitch	Turning Chain
Slip Stitch	0
Single Crochet	1
Half Double Crochet	2
Double Crochet	3
Treble Crochet	4
To make taller stitches, simply add one more chain for each subsequent stitch.	

Foundation Stitch Rows

Foundation stitch rows are especially useful when you need a stretchy foundation or when you want to add stitches at the end of a row. It's simple to work any stitch as a foundation stitch row. Begin with a starting chain that is the standard number of turning chains for that stitch plus one more. Be sure to include the required number of yarn overs for stitches taller than the single crochet, then insert the hook in the chain farthest from the hook. Draw a loop through the chain, yarn over and pull through the first loop on the hook to make one chain stitch, then complete the stitch as you would for the regular stitch.

> **TIP: Why Use a Foundation Stitch Row?**
> - It's stretchier and creates a more elastic edge.
>   - It's more efficient by combining the chain stitch and the first row of stitches in one.
> - It's easier to keep track of the number of stitches in the foundation row, especially on larger projects.
> - It's expandable because you can use the foundation stitch to add stitches at the end of a row.
> - It's adaptable because you can create a foundation stitch row using any of the basic stitches.

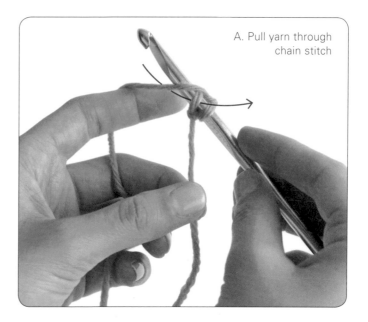

A. Pull yarn through chain stitch

Foundation Single Crochet (fsc)

The Foundation Single Crochet row combines the chain stitch with the first row of single crochet stitches.

1. Chain 2.

2. Insert the hook into the second chain from the hook, yarn over and pull a loop through the chain stitch (2 loops on hook; see photo A top right). Yarn over and pull through the first loop on the hook (see photo B bottom right; this forms 1 chain stitch at

B. Pull yarn through first loop on hook

the base of the row), yarn over and pull through both loops on the hook (1 fsc made; see photo C below).

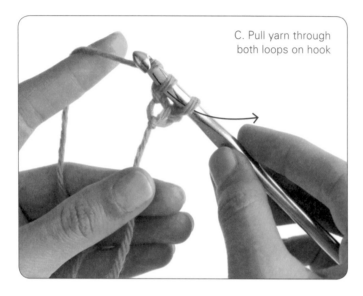

C. Pull yarn through both loops on hook

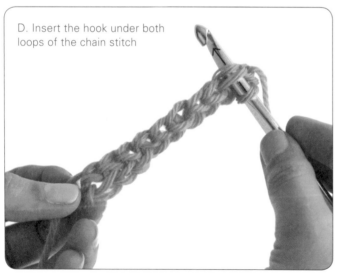

D. Insert the hook under both loops of the chain stitch

3. For the next fsc, insert the hook under both loops of the chain stitch found at the base of the last stitch worked (see photo D bottom left), yarn over and pull a loop through the chain stitch, yarn over and pull through the first loop on the hook, yarn over and pull through both loops on the hook.

4. Repeat step 3 for each fsc across.

Foundation Double Crochet (fdc)

The Foundation Double Crochet row combines the chain stitch with the first row of double crochet stitches.

1. Chain 4.

2. Yarn over and insert the hook into the fourth chain from the hook, yarn over and pull a loop through the chain stitch (3 loops on hook), yarn over and pull through the first loop on the hook (this forms 1 chain stitch at the base of the row), (yarn over and pull through the first two loops on the hook) twice (1 fdc made).

3. Yarn over and insert the hook under both loops of the chain stitch found at the base of the last stitch worked, yarn over and pull through the chain stitch, yarn over and pull through the first loop on the hook, (yarn over and pull through the first two loops on the hook) twice.

4. Repeat step 3 for each fdc across.

Single Crochet (sc)

To work a regular single crochet stitch, you will need to have a foundation row of stitches, like the chain stitch, to work into. If you begin with a row of Foundation Single Crochet (see page 21) skip to step 5.

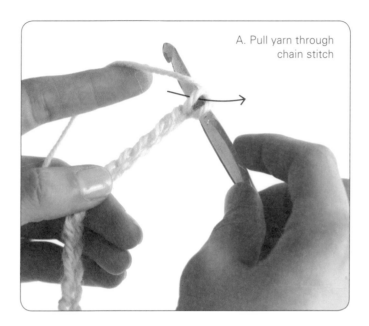

A. Pull yarn through chain stitch

1. Skip the first chain closest to the hook and insert the hook under the top loop of the second chain stitch.

2. Yarn over, catch the yarn with the hook, and pull a loop through the chain stitch (2 loops on hook; see photo A top right).

3. Yarn over and pull a loop through both loops on the hook (see photo B bottom right). Voilà—1 sc made.

4. Insert the hook under the top loop of the next chain and repeat steps 2 and 3 until you've worked 1 single crochet in each chain stitch across. When you've reached the end of the row, turn the work.

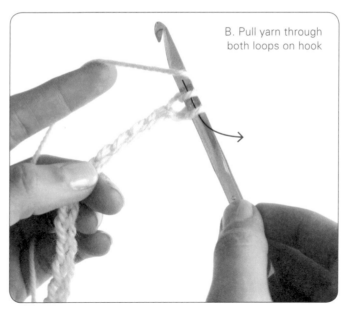

B. Pull yarn through both loops on hook

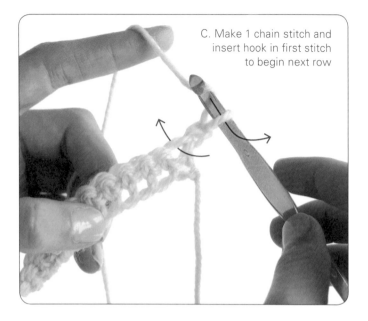

C. Make 1 chain stitch and insert hook in first stitch to begin next row

Half Double Crochet (hdc)

For stitches taller than a single crochet stitch, start with a yarn over before you insert the hook into the stitch on the previous row. The extra yarn over when working the half double crochet raises the stitch to about one and a half times the height of the single crochet stitch. If you begin with a row of Foundation Half Double Crochet (see page 20) skip to step 5.

5. Make 1 chain stitch and begin the next row by inserting the hook under both loops of the first stitch next to the hook (see photo C above). Yarn over, catch the yarn with the hook, and pull a loop through the first stitch (2 loops on the hook), yarn over and pull a loop through both loops on the hook.

6. Work 1 single crochet stitch in each stitch across, turn the work, and repeat step 5.

Be sure to count your stitches at the end of every row to make sure you aren't gaining or losing any. If you do find that your stitch count is changing, frog the piece and try again. If the problem persists, refer to Common Problems and How to Fix Them (page 52) for help.

1. Skip the first 2 chains closest to the hook, yarn over, and insert the hook under the top loop of the third chain stitch.

2. Yarn over, catch the yarn with the hook, and pull a loop through the chain stitch, leaving 3 loops on the hook (see photo A on page 25).

3. Yarn over and pull a loop through all 3 loops on the hook. You have made 1 half double crochet stitch (see photo B on page 25).

A. Pull yarn through chain stitch

4. Yarn over, insert the hook under the top loop of the next chain, and repeat steps 2 and 3 until you've worked 1 half double crochet in each chain stitch across. When you reach the end of the row, turn the work.

5. Make 2 chains for the turning chain and begin the next row. Yarn over and insert the hook under both loops of the second stitch (see photo C below). Yarn over, catch the yarn with the hook, and pull a loop through the stitch (3 loops on hook), yarn over and pull a loop through all 3 loops on the hook.

6. Work 1 half double crochet in each stitch across, turn the work, and repeat step 5.

B. Pull yarn through all 3 loops on work

C. Make 2 chains, yarn over, and insert the hook under both loops of the second stitch

Double Crochet (dc)

Start with a yarn over, work a few extra loops off the hook, and you'll end up with a tall stitch capable of producing light and lacy fabrics. The double crochet stitch is about twice the height of a single crochet. If you begin with a Foundation Double Crochet (see page 22) skip to step 5.

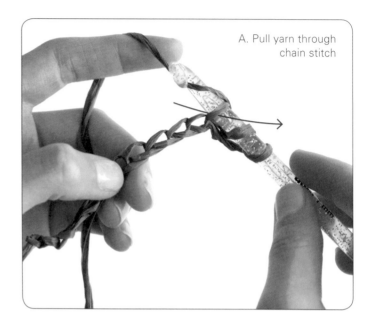

A. Pull yarn through chain stitch

1. Skip the 3 three chains closest to the hook, yarn over, and insert the hook under the top loop of the fourth chain stitch.

2. Yarn over, catch the yarn with the hook, and pull a loop through the stitch (see photo A top right; 3 loops on hook). Yarn over and pull a loop through the first 2 loops on the hook (see photo B bottom right; 2 loops on hook).

3. Yarn over and pull a loop through the remaining two loops on the hook. You have made 1 double crochet stitch (see photo C on page 27).

B. Pull yarn through first 2 loops on hook

C. Pull yarn through remaining 2 loops on hook

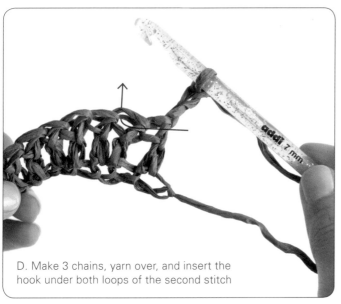

D. Make 3 chains, yarn over, and insert the hook under both loops of the second stitch

4. Yarn over, insert the hook under the top loop of the next chain, and repeat steps 2 and 3 until you've worked 1 double crochet in each chain stitch across. When you reach the end of the row, turn the work.

5. Make 3 chain stitches for the turning chain and begin the next row. Yarn over and insert the hook under both loops of the second stitch (see photo D bottom left). Yarn over, catch the yarn with the hook, and pull a loop through the stitch (3 loops on hook), yarn over and pull a loop through the first 2 loops on the hook (2 loops on hook), yarn over and pull a loop through the remaining 2 loops on the hook.

6. Work 1 double crochet stitch in each stitch across, turn the work, and repeat step 5.

Treble Crochet (tr)

With the treble crochet, we start with two yarn overs to get the stitch even taller than the double. If you begin with a Foundation Treble Crochet (see page 20) skip to step 6.

1. Skip the first 4 chains closest to the hook, yarn over 2 times, and insert the hook under the top loop of the fifth chain stitch from the hook.

2. Yarn over, catch the yarn with the hook, and pull a loop through the stitch (4 loops on hook). Yarn over and pull a loop through the first 2 loops on the hook (3 loops on hook).

3. Yarn over and pull a loop through the first 2 loops on the hook (2 loops on hook).

4. Yarn over and pull a loop through the remaining 2 loops on the hook (1 loop on hook). You have made 1 treble crochet stitch.

5. Yarn over 2 times, insert the hook under the top loop of the next chain, and repeat steps 2–4 until you've worked 1 treble crochet in each chain stitch across.

6. When you reach the end of the row, turn the work.

7. Make 4 chain stitches for the turning chain and begin the next row. Yarn over 2 times and insert the hook under both loops of the second stitch. Yarn over, catch the yarn with the hook, and pull a loop through the stitch, (yarn over and pull a loop through the first two loops on the hook) three times.

8. Work 1 treble crochet stitch in each stitch across, turn the work, and repeat step 6.

Slip Stitch (sl st)

The slip stitch is the shortest stitch of them all. Although you can use slip stitches to create firm fabric, they are more commonly used to join rounds, reduce a number of stitches, or make shaped edges. Because the slip stitch is so short, it doesn't require a turning chain when working a new row.

1. Insert the hook in the next stitch, yarn over, and pull a loop through the stitch and the loop on the hook in one move (see photo below).

2. Repeat step 1 for each slip stitch across.

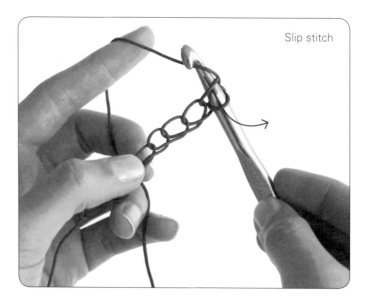

Slip stitch

Loops

Looking at the top of any stitch you'll see that each stitch has two strands that form the sides of a teardrop shape. These are known as the front loop and the back loop. When holding the fabric in front of you, the strand closest to you is the front loop and the strand farthest from you is the back loop. Unless a pattern instructs you to work in one loop or the other just go ahead and assume

Front loop

Back loop

you are supposed to insert the hook under both loops. Working under just one loop changes the texture of the pattern. For example, if you work a stitch using just the back loop you will create a fabric with a prominent rib-like texture of ridges and valleys that is very stretchy.

Post

Each stitch has a post, which is the body of the stitch connecting the loops at the top to the previous row of stitches. Post stitches are stitches worked around the post of the stitch from one, two, or three rows below. Post stitches are used to create dense, textured fabrics and belt-loop-style spaces, as in the Random Stripe Tote (page 111).

Spaces

The space in crocheted fabric is simply the space between stitches. Usually the space is created with one or more chain stitches in the previous row.

READING PATTERNS

If you've ever looked at a crochet pattern, you know how foreign the instructions can seem if you don't know how to read the abbreviations and instructions. Next up is a little section called Reading a Crochet Pattern 101. Let's take apart the different sections of the pattern from top to bottom.

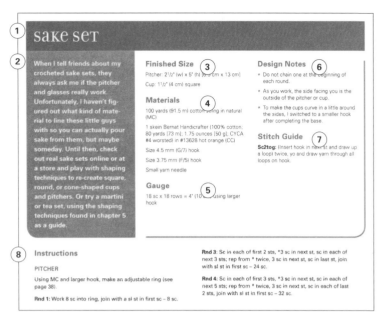

① sake set

② When I tell friends about my crocheted sake sets, they always ask me if the pitcher and glasses really work. Unfortunately, I haven't figured out what kind of material to line these little guys with so you can actually pour sake from them, but maybe someday. Until then, check out real sake sets online or at a store and play with shaping techniques to re-create square, round, or cone-shaped cups and pitchers. Or try a martini or tea set, using the shaping techniques found in chapter 5 as a guide.

Finished Size ③
Pitcher: 2¹/₂" (w) x 5" (h) (6.5 cm x 13 cm)
Cup: 1¹/₂" (4 cm) square

Materials ④
100 yards (91.5 m) cotton string in natural (MC)

1 skein Bernat Handicrafter (100% cotton; 80 yards (73 m); 1.75 ounces (50 g); CYCA #4 worsted) in #13628 hot orange (CC)

Size 4.5 mm (G/7) hook

Size 3.75 mm (F/5) hook

Small yarn needle

Gauge ⑤
18 sc x 18 rows = 4" (10 cm) using larger hook

Design Notes ⑥
• Do not chain one at the beginning of each round.
• As you work, the side facing you is the outside of the pitcher or cup.
• To make the cups curve in a little around the sides, I switched to a smaller hook after completing the base.

Stitch Guide ⑦
Sc2tog: (Insert hook in next st and draw up a loop) twice, yo and draw yarn through all loops on hook.

⑧ Instructions

PITCHER

Using MC and larger hook, make an adjustable ring (see page 38).

Rnd 1: Work 8 sc into ring, join with a sl st in first sc – 8 sc.

Rnd 3: Sc in each of first 2 sts, *3 sc in next st, sc in each of next 3 sts; rep from * twice, 3 sc in next st, sc in last st, join with sl st in first sc – 24 sc.

Rnd 4: Sc in each of first 3 sts, *3 sc in next st, sc in each of next 5 sts; rep from * twice, 3 sc in next st, sc in each of last 2 sts, join with sl st in first sc – 32 sc.

1. Pattern Title

2. Introduction

The introduction tells you what the project is, what inspired its design, and what it can be used for. This is also the place where I mention anything out of the ordinary that you need to know before you make the project, so be sure to scan this paragraph before you start.

3. Finished Size

The finished size represents the actual dimensions of the project as shown in the accompanying photograph. In other words, if you follow the gauge and use the same fiber I suggest, your finished project should be the same size shown. However, remember that any project can usually be adjusted to suit your needs. Look for ideas about altering the size of projects at the end of the pattern.

4. Materials

The materials section gives you a shopping list of fibers and tools used in the project. Ideas for substituting tools or materials to make the pattern more adaptable to your own stash and resources are in the Variations section at the end of the pattern instructions.

5. Gauge

Gauge is the number of stitches and rows measured within a 4-inch-square (10 cm) area on a 5-inch-square (13 cm) swatch (see page 34). The gauge of a fabric varies depend-

> **TIP:** You've decided to make a bag because you want one that looks just like it does in the photograph. Not only do you like the project, but you also want to make it *right now*. So you skip the gauge swatch, gather the materials as instructed, and begin to work. About halfway through the project, you realize that your bag doesn't look anything like the one in the photo. Maybe it's too stiff or too floppy or just not the size you expected it to be. Why is that? Well, gauge is a very individual thing, and the number of stitches and rows you make within a certain area may not be the number of stitches and rows I made when I designed the bag using the same hook and fiber. So even though it's a time-consuming activity, checking the gauge is the best way to ward off project disappointment.

ing on the fiber, hook size, stitch pattern, and tension. The main purpose for figuring out your gauge is to make certain your project will end up looking like the pattern pictured in the book. Taking time to create a small gauge swatch will save you the heartache of having to unravel your work or start over when you realize the gauge is off.

6. Design Notes

This section provides technical information specific to that pattern, for example: whether the turning chain is counted as a stitch at the end of the row or whether the work is turned at the end of a round.

7. Stitch Guide

This section explains how to work more complex stitches and stitch patterns.

8. Pattern Instructions

Crochet patterns are peppered with abbreviations and symbols that can read like an undecipherable code unless you know what everything means. The keys to the code follow.

ABBREVIATIONS

Commonly used stitches and terms are abbreviated to reduce the length of the pattern. Instead of *chain* you'll see *ch*, instead of *single crochet* you'll see *sc*. Terms

TIP: Crochet designers in North America use different terminology than designers in the United Kingdom, Australia, and Europe, so make sure you know the origin of your pattern before you start working. The patterns in this book use U.S. terms.

U.S.		U.K., Australia, Europe
slip stitch (sl st)	=	slip stitch (sl st)
single crochet (sc)	=	double crochet (dc)
half double crochet (hdc)	=	half treble crochet (htr)
double crochet (dc)	=	treble crochet (tr)

other than stitches that might be abbreviated include directions like repeat (*rep*), beginning (*beg*), and decrease (*dec*). See the list of abbreviations used in this book on page 157.

ASTERISKS, PARENTHESES, AND BRACKETS

Often a group of stitches, called a stitch pattern, will be repeated one or more times throughout the instructions. The repeat may be a group of stitches that are worked in a single stitch or across a whole row of stitches. Asterisks, parentheses, and brackets are used to identify the stitch pattern so you know exactly which stitches need to be repeated.

A single asterisk * identifies the starting point for the instructions to be repeated and a semicolon ; tells you where the repeat ends.

For example: *ch 3, sk 3 sts, dc in next ch-3 sp; rep from * across to end

Means: *Chain 3, skip the next 3 stitches, double crochet in the next chain 3 space, and repeat from the asterisk across to the end of the pattern

When only part of the instruction needs to be repeated, two asterisks will appear; one marks the start of the repeat and the other marks the end of the repeat.

For example: sc in each of next 10 sts, *ch 3, sk 3 sts, dc in next st*, sc in each of next 18 sts, rep from * to * once, sc in each st across to end

Means: Single crochet in each of the next 10 stitches, *chain 3, skip the next 3 stitches, double crochet in the next stitch*, single crochet in each of the next 18 stitches, repeat from the first asterisk to the second asterisk once, then single crochet in each stitch across to the end of the pattern

Parentheses are used to denote groups of stitches that are worked in the same stitch or space.

For example: dc in next st, ch 3, dc in same st

Could more easily be written as: (dc, ch 3, dc) all in same st

Brackets are used to denote a series of stitches that is worked in separate stitches or spaces and then repeated a certain number of times.

For example: ch 3, 3 dc into ring, ch 3, 3 dc into ring, ch 3, 3 dc into ring

Could more easily be written as: [ch 3, 3 dc into ring] 3 times

STITCH COUNTS

When following a pattern with lots of increases or decreases, you'll often see a stitch count given at the end of a row or round. Stitch counts are given whenever the total number of stitches has changed from the previous row or round. This helps you keep track of the shaping. Sometimes the turning chain is included in the stitch count and sometimes it isn't. Refer to the design notes at the beginning of the pattern for information about the turning chain.

FINISHING

This section of the pattern is about putting it all together. Here you'll find instructions on blocking; joining panels; adding straps, buttons, and closures; and installing a lining.

✳   ✳   ✳   ✳   ✳

Okay, that's it. Those are the basics, everything you need to know to start stitching a fabulous project. In the next chapter, I'll expand on the basics and discuss the fine points of completing a project, like how to shape the fabric, work in the round, join pieces, felt wool, and correct problems.

{ 3 }

TRYING NEW TECHNIQUES

Once you embrace the idea of uncommon crochet, you sign on for much more than simply crochet. When you add felting, sewing, embroidery, and loads of embellishments, the crochet fabric becomes a canvas for your personal creative expression. In this chapter, I talk about shaping, construction and finishing, fiber substitutions, and identifying and correcting the common mistakes that plague stitchers of all abilities.

SWATCH: THE "S" WORD

Swatch is a term that makes many people cringe because it's one extra little step between you and immediate project gratification. A swatch is simply a small sample of crocheted fabric that you create before you make a project to ensure that the fiber and hook you are using

produce the proper gauge. If the gauge in your swatch doesn't match the gauge in your pattern, your finished project won't turn out as expected.

If you're using the fiber that's called for in the pattern, but your gauge doesn't match, make a swatch with varying hook sizes until you get the gauge you're looking for. If you have to substitute a different fiber, make a swatch with the new fiber to make sure the hook you are using still produces the proper gauge. The swatch will also show you how the new fiber will behave in the pattern of stitches you are making. If you will eventually be starching, felting, or blocking your project, you can try it on your swatch first to make sure you get the results you want.

Swatches are also great for sampling new stitch patterns. As you learn the basic stitches, make practice swatches over and over until you can produce neat and uniform fabric.

To figure out whether you can make the same gauge as the one called for in the pattern, make a 5-inch-square (13 cm) swatch using the exact fiber in the pattern (or one that is similar in thickness and fiber content) and the suggested hook size and stitch pattern. To determine how many stitches are needed to make a 5-inch-square (13 cm) swatch, do a little simple math. If the gauge in the pattern says there should be 16 stitches over 4 inches (10 cm), then you know there are 4 stitches per inch (16 ÷ 4 = 4). To make the foundation chain, simply multiply the number of stitches per inch by how many inches you want the swatch to be: 4 stitches per inch x 5-inch swatch = 20 stitches. Then, work as many rows as it takes to make a 5-inch (13 cm) square and you're ready to check your gauge.

Measuring Your Gauge

Once your swatch is done, use your hands to smooth it out on a hard, flat surface. Using either a gauge tool, a stiff ruler, or a measuring tape, count the number of stitches across the center 4 inches (10 cm). Next, count how many rows you have within 4 inches (10 cm). These two numbers represent your gauge. The next step is to compare your gauge to the gauge listed in the pattern.

Most patterns specify a gauge over 4 inches (10 cm) to get an average number of stitches per inch, so why do I suggest that the swatch be at least 5 inches (13 cm)? The stitches at the edge of the swatch tend to be uneven

Swatch with a 4-inch square marked off to determine gauge

compared to the stitches in the center of the piece, so you need to add a few stitches at each edge of the swatch that won't be included in the gauge. Now, a 5-inch (13 cm) swatch may sound like a lot of wasted time and fiber, so if you must, go ahead and size it down to save time. Make the swatch 3 inches (7.5 cm) square, measure the stitches and rows within 2 inches (5 cm), then just double the number of stitches to figure out the gauge over 4 inches (10 cm), or cut it in half to figure out the per-inch gauge. It's your project, so you can make the swatch as big or as little as you want; the whole point is to get the most accurate information possible.

So, how close did your gauge come to the gauge listed in the pattern? If it's right on, then you're ready to start stitching. If your gauge is off the mark by even a quarter of an inch, then you'll need to make some adjustments.

Adjusting Your Gauge

Because gauge is dependent on the fiber, hook size, stitch pattern, and tension of the person creating it, there are a few ways you can adjust your gauge to hit the gauge required for the project.

1. If you're getting more stitches per inch than the pattern calls for, then your stitches are smaller than they should be. Try increasing the hook size to make bigger stitches.

2. If you're getting fewer stitches per inch than the pattern calls for, then your stitches are larger than they should be. Try decreasing the hook size to make smaller stitches.

3. If the pattern calls for a bulky fiber and your fiber is thin, try carrying more than one strand of fiber as you crochet to make the overall fiber thicker, or use a fiber with a thickness that is more suitable to the pattern.

4. If the pattern calls for a thin fiber and your fiber is bulky, choose another fiber because you won't be able to make it work with that particular pattern.

Once you've made some adjustments, crochet a new swatch and check your gauge again to make sure you match the gauge listed in the pattern.

SHAPING

One thing that sets crochet apart from knitting is how easy it is to sculpt the crocheted fabric into any shape or form. Shaping the fabric is simply a process of increasing or decreasing the number of stitches in a row or round to make it bigger or smaller. You control where the shaping takes place to create curves and dents as needed.

Increasing

To increase means to add stitches to make a section of the fabric bigger. You can add stitches by placing two or more stitches into one stitch or space (see photo A below) or by creating additional stitches at the beginning or end of a row. The patterns in this book will specify which of the above methods works best for that project.

To add multiple stitches at the beginning of a row, create one chain for each stitch you add (see photo B below right). Be sure to add the required number of chains for the turning chain (see chart on page 20) based on the stitch you're using, then skip the turning chain, work the first stitch in the following chain, and continue working across the chains and stitches from the previous row.

To add multiple stitches at the end of the row (see photo C on page 37), simply work one stitch into each stitch on the previous row as usual and then make the first additional stitch by inserting the hook into the vertical threads found at the base of the last stitch worked and work as a foundation stitch row (see page 20). Create another increase by working a foundation stitch into the chain found at the base of the foundation stitch row just completed. Continue working a foundation stitch for each increase as needed.

Decreasing

To decrease means to reduce stitches to make a section of the fabric smaller. You can decrease stitches by crocheting two or more stitches together, skipping stitches,

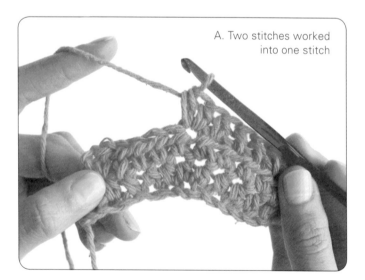

A. Two stitches worked into one stitch

B. Add chains to the beginning of the row

or leaving stitches unworked. The patterns in this book will specify which of the methods works best for that project.

To crochet two or more stitches together (see photo bottom right) work each stitch to the last step, leaving one additional loop on the hook. When you've worked each stitch to be decreased, yarn over and draw a loop through all the stitches on the hook.

To skip a stitch, you work in each stitch as usual until you come to the spot where you need to decrease. Decrease by skipping the stitch indicated, then work directly into the following stitch. You can skip one or more stitches at a time.

To decrease at the beginning of a row, you can work two stitches together, skip the first stitch, or work one slip stitch for each desired decrease. Slip stitches are not counted in the final row count, so do not work into the slip stitches on the return row.

To decrease at the end of a row, you can work two stitches together or simply stop and turn, leaving the desired number of decreases unworked.

Rows versus Rounds

In crochet, as in knitting, it's possible to work a piece in rows, meaning you work back and forth, turning the piece at the end of each row. Although working in rows is easy, working in the round is both easy and fun. When you work in the round, you open up a ton of creative possibilities in terms of the shapes you can create: circles, squares, tubes, triangles, and you name it can become bags, bowls, boxes, vases, and anything else you can imagine.

C. Hook inserted into the vertical threads at the base of the last stitch worked

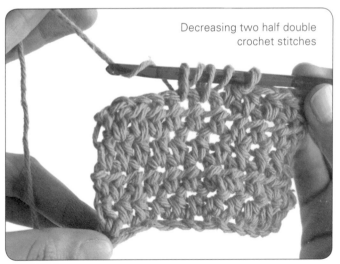

Decreasing two half double crochet stitches

When you work a project in the round, the first round is generally worked around a center stitch or space. This center stitch or space is created using one of two methods. For projects shaped like a tube (Lace Vases, page 149) or motifs (Corde Market Bag, page 139), start with a foundation ring, which has an open center. For projects that require a closed center like Red's Goodie Basket (page 95), start with an adjustable ring.

Foundation Ring (open center)

Start the circle by making your foundation row of chain stitches. Join the last chain to the first chain with a slip stitch to form a ring. The number of chain stitches in the foundation ring determines how large the center opening will be. Start with as little as three chain stitches to create a very small space in the center or start with ten or twenty chains to create a larger space in the center. The space can be left open to create lacy motifs or it can be functional and used as a buttonhole.

Adjustable Ring (closed center)

An adjustable ring is simply the beginning of a slip knot that hasn't been pulled tight into a knot. Work the first round of stitches into the open slip knot loop, then pull the tail end until the center is closed.

1. Leaving a 6-inch (15 cm) tail, wrap the yarn around two fingers to form a ring and use the hook to draw a loop up through the center of the ring. With the hook still in the loop, remove the ring from your

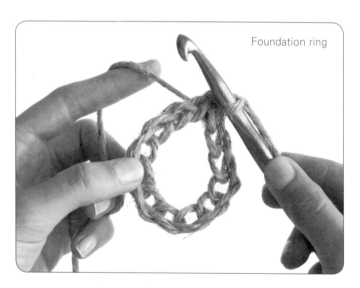

Foundation ring

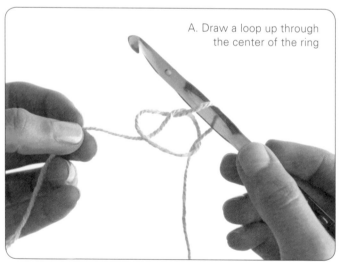

A. Draw a loop up through the center of the ring

fingers, grasp the ring with the left hand, and chain 1 (see photo A on page 38).

2. Make the required number of turning chains for the stitch you're creating and work the desired number of stitches into the ring (see photo B below).

3. Once you've made a round of stitches, pull the tail end to close the center of the circle (see photo C below right).

Once you have a foundation ring or an adjustable ring, you will continue to work in either a spiral or a joined round. Working in a spiral is perfect for projects where you don't want a visible seam (like Red's Goodie Basket, page 95). Working in joined rounds creates a

concentric pattern of circles with a seam line (like the Random Stripe Tote, page 111). If you are doing color work, join your rounds so you can complete one band of color on one round and start a new color on the next round. Changing colors while working in a spiral will create a zigzag where the color change occurs.

Joined Rounds

Working in joined rounds creates a seam along one side of the pattern by "joining" the last stitch of the round to the first stitch of the round with a slip stitch. You can affect the appearance of the seam by changing the direction in which you're working at the beginning of each round. If you join the end of the round and continue to

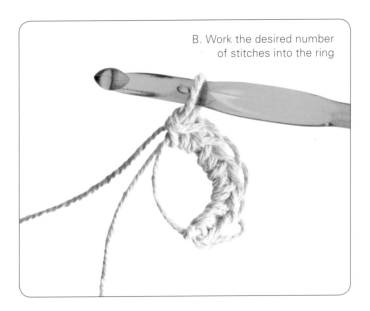

B. Work the desired number of stitches into the ring

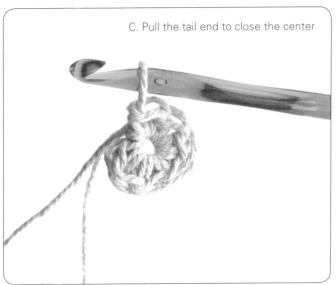

C. Pull the tail end to close the center

work the next round in the same forward direction, each row of stitches will look the same and your seam will travel diagonally along the work. However, if you join the end of the round and then turn the piece to work in the opposite direction, the rows change in appearance and you create a seam that runs straight up and down. If the project is long and thin, like the Lace Vases (page 149), a traveling seam might disrupt the project's appearance, so a vertical or invisible seam is more desirable. Sometimes the seam alignment is important and other times the texture and pattern created by working in the same or opposite directions is more important. The patterns in this book will indicate which method to use based on the needs of the project.

> **TIP:** The slip stitch at the end of each round is not considered a stitch unless otherwise instructed. If you work in joined rounds without turning at the end of each round, it is common to accidentally work an extra stitch into the slip stitch from the previous round. To help yourself learn to recognize the slip stitch, use stitch markers to mark the first and last stitch or count your stitches to make sure you aren't gaining any. If you are turning at the end of each round, simply skip the slip stitch from the previous round and begin the round in the next stitch.

Spiral

To work a spiral, you work in one continuous round without joining or making a turning chain. Working in a spiral creates a seamless fabric; however, it can be easy to lose track of how many rounds you've worked. To help keep track of the rounds, place a stitch marker in the first stitch of the first round. After you complete a full round, work the next stitch into the marked stitch, remove the marker, and move it to the new stitch you've just created.

WORKING IN THE TURNING CHAIN

When the turning chain counts as a stitch, you are usually required to work the last stitch of the next row or round into the turning chain. In this case, the pattern will instruct you to work the stitch into a specific chain of the turning chain.

For example: dc in 3rd ch of beg ch-5

Means: Double crochet into the third chain stitch of the turning chain that was made with 5 chains

To figure out which chain stitch you need to work into, begin counting the chain stitches at the base of the turning chain. Count chain stitches from the bottom up to find the chain you're supposed to work your stitch into. In the example above, you work a double crochet in the third chain from the bottom of the turning chain.

CHANGING FIBERS AND COLORS

To add a new fiber, work the last stitch with the old fiber until there are two loops left on the hook. Drop the old fiber to the back of the work and finish the stitch by pulling the new fiber through the remaining two loops (see photo below). Tug the old fiber to tighten it and then cut it, leaving a 4- to 6-inch (10 to 15 cm) tail. Continue to work using the new fiber.

Whenever possible, change fibers at the end of a row. Keeping your tail ends at the edges of the fabric makes it easier to hide them when you're finished and generally less conspicuous. There will of course be times when you need to change the fiber in the middle of the fabric. It's not a big deal, and you change the fiber the same way. In both methods, make sure the ends of both old and new fibers are at least 6 inches (15 cm) long so you can weave them in when you're finished. (See the tip in Weaving in Ends to learn how to hide the tail ends as you change the fiber.)

WEAVING IN ENDS

This is the process of tidying up all the loose fiber ends sticking out of your fabric when you finish the project. If done correctly, the tail ends will be hidden and your work will look neat and polished. Use a yarn or tapestry needle to weave in the tail ends with most fibers. Leather cord and wire can simply be woven in with your fingers or pulled through stitches with a crochet hook.

To weave in your ends:

- If the tail end comes out at the top or bottom edges of the work, weave it in under both loops of the stitches.

- If the tail end comes out along the side edges, or row ends, of the fabric, weave it vertically through the threads along the edge.

- If the tail end comes out somewhere within the fabric, weave it horizontally or vertically through the posts (see page 29) of the stitches. Either way, weave the tail on the wrong side (see page 16) or back of the work.

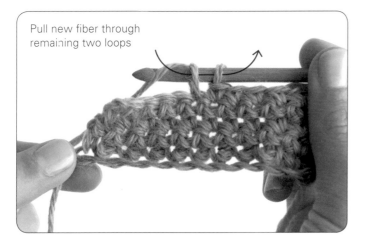

Pull new fiber through remaining two loops

To make the finishing process easy and virtually invisible:

- Leave a 6-inch (15 cm) tail at the beginning of the work and any time you start or end a fiber along the way. Short tails are difficult to hide and tend to stick out of the fabric.

- Start a new ball of fiber at the edge of the work whenever possible.

- Never tie the tail ends into knots. Knots leave a conspicuous bump in the fabric.

- If there is already a knot in the fiber from the manufacturer, cut the knot out, leaving a 6-inch (15 cm) tail, and then start the new strand of fiber.

- Weave in your ends as you go (see the Tip below) to make the finishing process quick and easy.

TIP: To save yourself time at the end of a project, weave the tails in as you go. It may feel a little awkward at first, but after some practice you'll do it automatically. To weave in the beginning tail of a new fiber, lay the new fiber on top of the previous row a few inches before you need it. Continue to stitch with the old fiber, working over the new tail to conceal it. Complete the fiber switch as usual. If you don't need the old fiber any longer, fasten it off and leave a few inches for the tail end. Lay the tail end on top of the previous row and continue stitching with the new fiber, working over the old tail to conceal it.

FELTING

What most people call *felting* is actually the process of *fulling*. The difference between the two terms refers to whether or not the fibers have been worked up into a piece of fabric before being agitated in hot water. Fulling is shrinking a piece of fabric that has been crocheted, woven, or knit, while felting is shrinking loose pieces of animal fiber, like roving. For the sake of familiarity, I refer to the process of shrinking crocheted fabric as felting (but at least now you know the real meanings!). The key elements of felting are heat, soap, water, and agitation. The water must be hot and soapy to get the fibers to open up, and the agitation is necessary for encouraging the fibers to tangle and lock together.

The cool thing about felting is that it will completely transform a project from something big and loose and possibly unattractive into something beautiful and functional. It also hides mistakes. If you have a hole in the fabric or forgot to make a few decreases, it will all be covered up in the wash. After it's shrunk to the desired size, you can stretch, smooth, and shape most mistakes right out of the fabric.

More information about how to design your own felted projects is on page 124.

Felting FAQ

What types of yarn will felt? You can only felt yarns that are made of untreated animal fibers, such as alpaca, sheep, rabbit, and even dog fur. Wools that say *superwash* on the label cannot be felted because they have been treated to prevent felting in the wash. You can try to felt blended yarns containing only a percentage of animal fiber, but I recommend that you felt a test swatch first to make sure you'll get your desired result. Note that not all yarns felt in the same way: some felt more quickly and others felt with more texture.

What if I'm using a different yarn than is called for in a pattern? If you need to substitute a yarn and the finished size of the project is important, always felt a test swatch of the new yarn. Some yarns yield drastically different results than others. Refer to the tips on designing your own felted project (see page 124) to learn more about making substitute yarn work in any project.

What size hook should I use? To have room to shrink, your stitches must be loose, so use a larger hook size than what is normally recommended for the yarn when you plan to felt your project. All of the projects in this book will direct you to the proper hook size for successful felting.

How much will the fabric shrink? The longer you wash the item, the more it will shrink. Generally I've found that crocheted fabric shrinks anywhere from 15 to

Swatch before and after felting

35 percent, and it's unlikely that the width and length will shrink evenly. The only way to know how a particular yarn will react is to felt a test swatch.

Can I put a felted project in the dryer? Putting a felted project in the dryer may help remove excess water and shorten the drying time; however, the dryer may also cause warps or creases.

Can I felt lace or textured stitch patterns? Basic stitch patterns deliver the best results when felting. Lace and textured stitch patterns get lost in felted fabric. Remember to felt a test swatch when you're using a new stitch pattern to make sure you get your desired result.

How do I keep edges from stretching? Open edges tend to stretch more in the wash than edges that have been joined together. To keep any unattached edges from felting unevenly use a cotton fiber either to loosely baste them or to work a row of single crochet along the edge.

Can I change the thickness of the fabric? The easiest way to adjust the thickness of a finished fabric is to change the stitch or yarn weight before you felt. Try working with a double strand of wool to create a thick fabric or working in the front loop only to create a thin fabric.

How can I find out whether my unlabeled stash yarn will felt? Wrap the yarn around your fingers a few times and break it off. Dip the loop in a bowl of hot water with a little soap and rub it quickly between your hands. If it gets fuzzy and tangled together, it's good to go. If you can restore the yarn to its original condition, put it back in the stash.

Can I cut felted fabric? Yep. Cut, sew, glue, embroider, bead—whatever you want, it should hold together.

How to Felt

To felt your crocheted project in the washing machine:

1. Place your project in a zippered laundry bag or pillowcase and either zip it closed or close it tightly with a rubber band. Encasing the project in a bag will keep lumps of wool from bunching up in the machine.

2. Set the machine to the smallest load setting, the hot wash, and the cold rinse. Heat is essential to the felting process, so if you don't think the water is getting hot enough, add a pot of boiling water to turn it up a notch.

3. Put three to four tablespoons of baking soda or a small amount of detergent in the machine and add an old pair of jeans, a shoe, or a rubber ball to increase agitation. Check the machine often (to keep it from moving on to the rinse and spin cycles) until your project reaches the desired size and texture. I leave the machine lid open so I can reset the wash cycle as many times as necessary until it's done.

4. Remove your project from the bag and gently roll it in a towel to remove the excess water.

5. Remove any basting stitches and shape your project by pulling and smoothing out any warps or wrinkles. Insert a form if necessary to help the object keep its shape while it dries.

To felt your crocheted project by hand:

Using hot, soapy water, vigorously scrub the project until it's felted to the desired consistency. To increase the agitation, scrub the piece on a bamboo sushi mat or washboard. Felt small pieces, projects with raw edges that have been cut, or spots that need extra attention by hand. Note that felting by hand will take a little longer than felting by machine and it will leave your hands in desperate need of moisturizer.

BLOCKING

Blocking is a simple finishing technique that helps shape and relax a piece of crocheted fabric to prepare it for assembly or give the final project a neat and polished appearance. Blocking lets you stretch and shape the fabric, smooth out the stitches, neaten up the edges, and relax stiff, crunchy, and curly fibers. While there are several ways to block your work, the basic steps for all methods include:

1. Wetting the fiber.

2. Stretching and shaping the pieces to the desired size, using a form if necessary.

3. Allowing the piece to dry.

To successfully block a project, you need a few tools: a blocking surface, water, rust-proof pins, a ruler, and a form (if necessary for shaping; see below). The blocking surface should be flat, something you can stick pins into, and something that can get wet. You can purchase a blocking board, which is made specifically for the process, or you can create your own surface by folding up a towel or using an ironing board. (I used a towel when blocking most of the projects in this book.) If you don't use a blocking board, which has a grid of ruled lines to make uniform shaping easier, use a ruler to measure the piece when you're blocking to a certain size.

Different fibers prefer different methods of blocking. If the fiber you're using doesn't come with a wash-and-care label, use the methods below as a guide or block a small sample swatch before you block the finished project to make sure you get the desired result.

Wet Blocking

The wet block method soaks the fabric to relax sturdy fibers like jute, hemp, and sisal. Although plant fibers tend to be stiff and inelastic in their natural state, a simple wet block can give the project a softer drape. Animal fibers may also be wet blocked to give the project a polished appearance, but handle them gently because they tend to felt in the presence of heat and agitation. Do not wet block delicate fibers like silk, which may fall apart or become water damaged.

To wet block:

1. Submerge the piece in a bowl, sink, or tub of cool water, and then gently roll it in a towel to remove the excess water. Do not wring.

2. Lay the piece on a flat blocking surface, shape it to the desired size, and pin the edges to the blocking surface.

3. Allow the piece to dry completely. Drying time can be a few hours to several days depending on the thickness of the fiber.

Steam Blocking

The steam block method, which uses steam to relax and soften the fabric, is the most versatile process because it works well on most fibers, including those that shouldn't get thoroughly wet. Be very careful when steam blocking synthetic fibers, as they can become scorched with too much heat. You will need a fabric steamer or an iron with a steam setting. Do not let the steam touch the fabric directly.

To steam block:

1. Lay the piece on a flat blocking surface, shape it to the desired size, and pin the edges to the blocking surface.

2. Move the steamer (or a steam iron set to steam) 5 to 10 inches (13 to 25.5 cm) above the fabric until the entire piece is damp. Alternatively, you could thoroughly wet a thin towel or piece of linen, wring it out to remove the excess water, and lay this over the pinned piece. Then press lightly on the towel with a steam iron until the entire piece is damp. Remove the towel.

3. Allow the piece to dry completely. Drying time can be a few hours to several days depending on the thickness of the fiber.

Spray Blocking

The spray block method is the gentlest process, using a misting of water to relax the fabric for a nice drape. This method is best for delicate fibers like silk, any fiber that can't be wet or steam blocked, and projects that only require light blocking to shape the piece. You will need a spray bottle filled with water.

To spray block:

1. Lay the piece on a flat blocking surface, shape it to the desired size, and pin the edges to the blocking surface.

2. Mist the fabric evenly with water until damp.

3. Allow the piece to dry completely. Drying time can be a few hours to several days depending on the thickness of the fiber.

Forms

Some projects, like felted bags or starched containers, need to be formed into a three-dimensional shape while they dry. The trick is to find an object that has the shape or dimension you want for your project. To block with a form, insert the form into the piece, wet the piece according to the blocking method you are using, stretch the fabric around the form to achieve the desired shape, and then set it aside to dry completely. If you are using objects as forms that really shouldn't get wet, like your brother's favorite DVD or the book you just borrowed from a friend, place the object in a plastic bag before you block.

Here are a few ideas for forms you might be able to find around the house:

- Plastic drawers, boxes, or containers

- Wadded-up plastic grocery bags

- Plastic canvas (the stuff used for cross-stitch or needlepoint is also used to give bags or boxes structure; find it at craft stores); cut or bend it to shape

- Balloons

- Bowls, glasses, or bottles

- Wadded-up newspaper

- DVDs

- Books: hardcovers, paperbacks, phone, or other

JOINING PANELS

There are a few methods for joining crocheted fabrics together. You can stitch them together with fiber and a needle, crochet them together with a hook, or sew them together with a sewing machine. Whether the seam is visible or not depends on which way the fabrics are held together during the seaming process. If you join the pieces with the right sides of the fabric together, you will end up with a virtually invisible seam. If you hold the wrong sides of the fabric together, the seam will be visible from the outside. Intentionally working the seam so it's visible from the outside is usually done for decorative reasons. Work under at least two threads for each layer of fabric to ensure that the seam is secure. This creates a bulkier seam than if you worked under just one loop, but you don't want your seams stretching.

You can use a variety of common sewing stitches to create a seam. I usually use the backstitch, whipstitch, running stitch, or basting stitch. Any of these stitches can be worked in thread, yarn, or fiber. The size of the needle you need depends on the thickness of the fiber and the type of fabric you're working with. The needle should be able to sew through the fabric without stretching it and the eye of the needle should be large enough to accommodate the thread or fiber. Before you start stitching, secure the fiber (do this at the end of your seam, too) by sewing a few short stitches in the same location, working over the tail end to keep it in place. If you are sewing with a thick fiber, you can weave in the tail ends instead (see page 41).

Backstitch

The backstitch is often used to create invisible seams along the inside (or wrong side) of the fabric. This method creates a secure, inelastic seam because each stitch overlaps the previous one. Use the backstitch for seams that require strength.

1. Pin the pieces together with right or wrong sides facing according to the pattern instructions. Be sure to align the edges of the pieces, with rows or stitch patterns lining up.

2. Cut and thread an 18-inch (46 cm) length of fiber onto your needle. With one side of the fabric facing you, bring the needle from back to front through all layers.

3. Take a small stitch 1/4 inch (0.5 cm) back, pushing the needle from front to back, then bring the needle from back to front 1/2 inch (1 cm) forward.

4. Repeat step 3 along the seam.

Whipstitch

The whipstitch looks like the spiral binding of a book. It can be used for an inside seam or to create a decorative edge on an outside seam. The whipstitch creates a more flexible seam than the backstitch.

1. Pin the pieces together with right or wrong sides facing according to the pattern instructions. Be sure to align the edges of the pieces, with rows or stitch patterns lining up.

2. Cut and thread an 18-inch (46 cm) length of fiber onto your needle. With one side of the fabric facing you, bring the needle from back to front through all layers.

Backstitch

Whipstitch

3. Bring the needle over the top of both edges and insert it from back to front again, through all layers, about 1/4 inch (0.5 cm) further along the fabric.

4. Repeat step 3 along the seam.

Running and Basting Stitches

The running stitch is one of the most basic stitches in sewing. It's used for gathering fabric, decorative outlining, making temporary seams (also known as basting), and sewing basic seams that won't take too much strain. Running stitches are spaced 1/8 to 1/4 inch (0.3 to 0.5 cm) apart for seaming. Basting stitches are simply longer running stitches, spaced 1/2 to 3/4 inch (1 to 2 cm) apart.

Running stitch

Basting stitches are used to temporarily hold fabrics together or to mark a stitching line.

1. Pin the pieces together with right or wrong sides facing according to the pattern instructions. Be sure to align the edges of the pieces, with rows or stitch patterns lining up.

2. Cut and thread an 18-inch (46 cm) length of fiber onto your needle.

3. With one side of the fabric facing you and working from right to left, weave the point of the needle in and out of the fabric, through all layers. Keep the stitches even and consistent, placing the same amount of space between each one.

Joining with a Hook

The most common method of crocheting pieces together is to work a slip stitch or single crochet through both layers of fabric. You can also join pieces together with chain stitches (as described in the Corde Market Bag on page 139). A crocheted seam can be worked on the right sides of the fabric to create a decorative and visible seam (see the Vintage Satchel on page 73), or from the wrong side so the seam is hidden (as in the Jute Filet Bag on page 69). Unless otherwise instructed, always work under at least two threads for each layer of fabric to make the seam secure.

Slip Stitch

Joining pieces together with a slip stitch creates a strong, inelastic seam.

1. Pin the pieces together with right or wrong sides facing according to the pattern instructions. Be sure to align the edges of the pieces, with rows or stitch patterns lining up.

2. With one side of the fabric facing you, join yarn by bringing a loop through the first stitch from both layers from back to front with the hook. Pull the tail end to 4 to 6 inches (10 to 15 cm) to the back and hold it out of the way for weaving in later.

3. Insert the hook from front to back, through both layers, 1/4 to 1/2 inch (0.5 to 1 cm) farther along the fabric, yarn over, and pull a loop through to the front, then through the loop on the hook.

4. Repeat step 3 along the seam. Fasten off and weave in ends.

Single Crochet

Joining pieces with single crochet creates a flexible, ridged seam that can be used for decorative purposes when worked on the right sides of the project.

1. Pin the pieces together with right or wrong sides facing according to the pattern instructions. Be sure to align the edges of the pieces, with rows or stitch patterns lining up.

2. With one side of the fabric facing you, join yarn by bringing a slip knot through the first stitch from back to front with the hook. Pull the tail end 4 to 6 inches (10 to 15 cm) to the back and either hold it out of the way for weaving in later or lay it on top of the fabric edges so you can work over it as you join them together.

3. Yarn over and pull a loop through the loop on the hook.

4. Insert the hook from front to back, through both layers, 1/4 to 1/2 inch (0.5 to 1 cm) farther along the fabric. Yarn over and pull a loop through to the front (2 loops on hook), yarn over and pull through both loops on the hook.

5. Repeat step 4 along the seam. Fasten off and weave in ends.

ADDING LININGS

I love to make bags with stylish linings, but my first attempts at sewing were crude at best. I broadened my creative horizons by learning hand- and machine-sewing skills, so if you don't have a lot of sewing experience, here are a few tips for preparing and sewing woven fabrics to your crocheted projects.

- Prewash fabrics to remove excess dyes and to avoid shrinkage after you've sewn it into your project.

- Always measure everything twice.

- To make sturdy seams, use a backstitch (see page 47) or a combination of a few running stitches (see page 49) and a backstitch.

- Finger press or iron the seam allowances flat before you sew the seam. Pressing the hem can be used as a substitute or in addition to using pins, but it helps keep the edges from sliding out of place while you work.

- Get yourself some fusible webbing. It is a piece of fiber that fuses fabrics together to hold them in place before sewing and to add stability to lighter weight fabrics.

EMBELLISHING YOUR PROJECTS

Many of the patterns in this book feature embellishments that make the project unique. Buttons, beads, and ribbons are embellishments that you can find in most craft stores. Felted beads (see page 154) and embroidered stitches are embellishments that you can create yourself. Embroidery may look difficult at first, but the basic stitches—running stitch, backstitch, and whipstitch—are easy to master with a little practice. Decorative stitches, like the blanket stitch and French knot, are described in patterns throughout the book. I learned most of my embroidery skills through books and websites with lots of pictures and video stitch guides. *The Readers Digest Complete Guide to Needlework* (Readers Digest, 1979) has step-by-step instructions, photographs, and illustrations for all types of needlework, including sewing, crochet, knitting, macramé, quilting, appliqué, and embroidery. Check it out.

SUBSTITUTING YARNS AND FIBERS

Although many projects in this book were designed to be made with nontraditional fibers, you can pretty easily substitute more mainstream yarns if you choose.

When substituting yarns and fibers in these patterns—or in any pattern—choose an alternate fiber that is similar in content, texture, and thickness. For instance, string and cotton yarns are very similar in size and fiber content, so they are easily interchangeable. Sisal, on the other hand, is a highly textured, thick twine. If you tried to substitute it for a cotton project like the Strappy Clutch (page 107), you would end up with an unpleasantly rough and large clutch.

Once you've selected a fiber, create a sample swatch using the suggested hook size to determine whether the fiber is suitable for the pattern. First compare your gauge to the pattern gauge. If the gauge matches, you can move on to drape. If the gauge is off, try a new hook size until you get the gauge needed for the pattern. If the gauge is way off, you may want to reconsider the new fiber.

Once the question of gauge has been settled, assess the swatch for drape. Drape is a term that describes the way a fabric hangs. If you think about the drapes or curtains in your living rooom, you can imagine how the word applies to crocheted fabric. A soft and lacy bag with fluidity in its structure is considered to have better drape than a container with stiff sides. The content, texture, and thickness of a fiber affect how the finished fabric will drape. An animal fiber like wool is soft and stretchy; it is more likely to produce a fabric with better drape than the same pattern made with a strong, inelastic plant fiber like cotton. A thick fiber with lots of texture like sisal will produce a stiff and rigid fabric with considerably less drape than a smooth and slick fiber like string or thin leather cord.

If your gauge is off and the fiber is wrong, the drape of the project changes and you won't end up with what you expect. Even if the gauge is right, the fiber still may not produce the intended drape. For example, if you're making a container that stands up on its own, you need tight stitches and a strong fiber. Big, loose stitches and a soft, limp fiber won't give you the desired drape. Changing the hook size can alter how a fabric drapes. If the fabric isn't behaving the way you want it to, try changing the size of the hook. Go up in size for a looser stitch and more drape, or go down in size for a tighter stitch and less drape. (For more information about drape, see page 82.)

If the new yarn or fiber has the proper gauge and a similar drape, it's suitable for the project and you're good to go.

common problems and HOW TO FIX THEM

This section addresses a few of the most common problems you'll run into when crocheting, why they happen, and—most important—how to fix them.

The Problem: The edges of the fabric are getting narrower.

What's Happening? You've lost stitches somewhere along the way.

Why? Stitches are commonly lost at the beginning or end of a row because it's hard to tell where the first or last stitch of the row is.

To Fix It: Count the number of stitches in the row. If you've lost several stitches and it's noticeable, hold up the piece and try to figure out where it started to narrow, then go ahead and carefully pull out the stitches to that point. Count the number of stitches in that row and if you have the right number of stitches, begin to stitch again.

If you've only lost one or two stitches, work the next row with the same number of increases (see page 36) to get you back on track. Hold up the work and see whether the fix is noticeable. If it's not, then do your best to forget about it. If it is, see above.

To keep the problem from happening in the future, use a stitch marker to mark the first and last stitch of the row. When you work your way back to the marker you'll know where to place your first or last stitch. Count the stitches in the row every few inches to make sure you have them all.

The Problem: The edges of the fabric are getting wider.

What's Happening? You've added stitches somewhere along the way.

Why? Stitches are commonly added at the beginning or end of a row because it's hard to tell where the first or last stitch of the row is.

To Fix It: Count the number of stitches in the row. If you've added several stitches and it's noticeable, hold up the piece and try to figure out where it started to get wider, then go ahead and carefully pull out the stitches to that point. Count the number of stitches in that row and if you have the right number of stitches, begin to stitch again.

If you've only added one or two stitches, work the next row with the same number of decreases (see page 36) to get you back on track. Hold up the work and see whether the fix is noticeable. If it's not, then do your best to forget about it. If it is, see above.

To keep the problem from happening in the future, use a stitch marker to mark the first and last stitch of the row. When you work your way back to the marker you'll know where to place your first or last stitch. Count the stitches in the row every few inches to make sure you have them all.

The Problem: The edges of the fabric are curling.

What's Happening? The tension in the stitches may be too tight or the content of the fiber may just create a stiff fabric.

Why? There are two reasons why your tension may be too tight. (1) You may be pulling the working yarn too tightly as you work the stitches, or (2) the hook size is too small for the fiber.

To Fix It: Try stretching the work to see whether it loosens up the stitches.

Loosen up your tension. Try changing the way you hold the working yarn. If you are wrapping the yarn around the pinkie or index finger more than once, take off a loop to allow the yarn to flow more smoothly.

Try working with a larger hook size.

Block it. If you are just too far gone and the piece is almost done, try blocking it to reduce the curl.

The Problem: The foundation edge is narrower or tighter than the rest of the fabric.

What's Happening? The foundation chain stitches are too tight.

Why? The chain stitch is narrow and doesn't have the supporting threads that bigger stitches have, so it's easy to make the foundation chain too tight.

To Fix It: Try to keep the chain stitches loose. Some of the slack in the stitch will be taken up by the following row of stitches.

If you have trouble adjusting your chain tension, try using a hook one size larger to make the chain, then switch back to the project hook on the following row.

Use the foundation stitch rows (see page 20) to create a foundation edge that is more even with the rest of the work.

The Problem: There are gaps along the edges of the work.

What's Happening? The turning chain may be too loose.

Why? Sometimes the standard turning chain doesn't work well with the fiber or your particular tension.

To Fix It: Omit one chain from the standard turning chain for the stitch you are using.

The Problem: I'm struggling to slide the hook through the stitches.

What's Happening? Your tension is too tight or the hook is pointing in the wrong direction.

Why? Holding the fiber too tightly and pointing the grooved end of the hook in the wrong direction are common mistakes for beginning crocheters.

To Fix It: Try loosening up the amount of tension applied with the hand controlling the yarn.

Be sure to point the grooved end of the hook toward the inside point of the stitch.

Keep the chain stitches loose and fat. Any slack in the stitch will be taken up by the following row of stitches.

{ 4 }

create
Simple Projects to Spark Your Creativity

Sometimes the easiest way to spark your creativity is to make an existing pattern. As you work, think about ways you could change the pattern to suit your personality by making it bigger or smaller, changing the stitch pattern or fiber, or adding embellishments. I use this approach with cooking. I'll follow a recipe the first time, then start adding and subtracting ingredients based on my likes and dislikes—and sometimes my empty pantry. It's true that occasionally I end up with a culinary disaster, but more often than not, I discover a new and tasty dish.

In "Create," I offer up some very basic patterns using simple stitches and techniques. If you like the projects as they are, go ahead and follow the instructions to make what you see in the photos. If you want to customize the project to your own taste, I've included ideas for tweaking the original project—to adjust the size or fiber—at the end of the pattern.

With the Tube Bag (page 57), you'll learn to use basic stitches and felting to create a fashionable bag with very little construction. I follow the main pattern with three easy adaptations to get you started customizing your own projects. The Jute Filet Bag (page 69) uses a sturdy fiber and introduces the concept of adding a simple lining. With the Vintage Satchel (page 73), you will play with variations on a basic stitch and practice sewing pieces together. In the Patchwork Handbag (page 77), you will work up crocheted squares using uncomplicated stitches, then combine them with squares of fabric and a lining.

Start with the basic project, and then let your creativity run wild. In the next chapter, I'll talk about the basic principles of designing a project, including specific techniques for shaping and embellishing.

THE TUBE BAG

This bag is created from a simple tube, a basic shape with many possible adaptations. To complete the bag, you need to know how to do a chain stitch, half double crochet, and slip stitch—that's it! After felting, simply assemble by sewing the straps to the felted bag. The basic tube bag pattern is followed by three variations. The Hong Kong Bag (page 59) includes a flap, grommets with leather lacing, and recycled leather shoulder straps. The Flower Basket Bag (page 63) has crocheted handles, increase shaping, and flower embellishments. The Window Bag (page 65) uses cutouts to create a handle and little windows to show off a special lining.

Finished Size

Before felting: 14" (w) x 12" (h) [35.5 cm x 30.5 cm], excluding handles

After felting: 9¹/2" (w) x 9" (h) [24 cm x 23 cm]

Materials

2 skeins Berroco Ultra Alpaca (50% alpaca, 50% wool; 215 yards [198 m]; 3.5 ounces [100 g]; CYCA #4 worsted) in #6248 pastel yellow

Size 5.5 mm (I/9) hook

2 yards (2 m) scrap cotton yarn or thread in any color

Large-eyed yarn needle

Form to fit finished dimensions of bag, such as plastic-wrapped book or DVD case

2 yards (2 m) 1¹/2- to 2-inch-wide (4 to 5 cm) ribbon in gold and blue pattern, for the straps

4 Dritz metal 1¹/4-inch (3 cm) D-rings in gold

Sewing needle

Thread to match the ribbon

Gauge

14 hdc x 8 rows = 4" (10 cm)

Design Notes

- Working in the front loop only creates a thin felted fabric.
- This pattern is worked in a spiral, which means the rounds will not be joined. Just keep going and going and going until the bag is the correct size.
- The foundation chain and whipstitch seam should be done loosely so there is room in the stitches to shrink evenly along with the rest of the fabric.
- Folding in the bottom corners of the bag will create a paper bag–like fold at the bottom for added strength.
- Basting the opening of the bag before washing will keep the open edges from stretching out of shape.

Stitch Guide

Hdc-flo: Half double crochet through front loop only.

Instructions

Loosely ch 100, sl st in first ch to form a ring.

Hdc-flo in each ch around, do not join in the first st. Continue working hdc-flo in each st around in a spiral until piece measures 12 inches (30.5 cm) from foundation ch. Sl st in next st. Fasten off and continue to Finishing or one of the following adaptations to customize your bag.

Finishing

Turn the bag inside out. Pressing the tube flat, join yarn through both layers of the first st on one end and slip stitch the tube together to form the bottom. Fold the bottom corner points in 1 inch (2.5 cm) with the tip of the point aligned with the seam and sew a couple of stitches to secure (see photo below). This creates a paper bag–like base for the bag. Turn the bag right side out. Thread the scrap cotton yarn onto yarn needle and baste (see page 49) the opening of the bag closed. Follow the instructions on page 44 for felting in the washing

machine. Once the bag has felted to size, roll it in a towel to remove the excess water and then remove the basting thread. Insert the form and set the bag in a warm and dry area to dry completely (this may take up to a couple of days).

Cut two long pieces of ribbon to 22 inches (56 cm) and two short pieces to 14 inches (35 cm). To attach the D-rings, thread the end of one long piece through one D-ring, fold the end over 1/4 inch (0.5 cm) twice to hide the raw edge, and sew the hem close to the D-ring. Add a D-ring to the three remaining ends of the two long pieces of ribbon in the same manner. Next, attach one end of a short piece of ribbon to the attached D-ring of a long piece of ribbon and attach the second end of the short piece to a D-ring on the second long piece of ribbon. Repeat for the second short piece of ribbon until all pieces are connected in an oval.

The short ribbon pieces will make up the handles of the bag, and the long ribbon pieces are sewn to the bag. Wrap the long ribbons around the front, bottom, and back of the bag about 1 inch (2.5 cm) in from the sides. Sew the ribbons in place using 1/8-inch backstitches and matching thread.

Variation

To substitute the yarn, use 325 yards (297 m) of 100 percent animal fiber in a worsted weight; do not use superwash.

To make the bag wider, add stitches to the foundation chain.

To make the bag longer, add additional rounds.

HONG KONG BAG

The idea for this bag started with a coin my mom brought me from Hong Kong. I knew the coin wanted to be a button closure. This bag has it all—felting, grommets, lacing, and my very first attempts at embroidery (see the variation below).

Finished Size

Before felting: 14" (w) x 12" (h) [35.5 cm x 30.5 cm], excluding handles

After felting: 9¹⁄₂" (w) x 8" (h) [24 cm x 20 cm]

Materials

2 skeins Brunswick Yarns Germantown Knitting Worsted (100% pure virgin wool; 265 yards [242 m]; 4 ounces [114 g]; CYCA #4 worsted) in #474 brick heather

Size 5.5 mm (I/9) hook

Large-eye yarn needle

1 yard (1 m) scrap cotton yarn or thread in any color

Form to fit finished dimensions of bag, such as plastic-wrapped book or DVD case

Pins

1 (15-inch-long [38 cm]) recycled leather strap or store-bought bag strap

Sewing needle

Thread to match the strap

Knitting needle or screwdriver

Small scissors

4 (⁷⁄₁₆-inch [1 cm]) grommets in antique brass

1¹⁄₂ yards (137 cm) ¹⁄₈-inch-wide (3 mm) leather lacing in dark brown

1 (1-inch [2.5 cm]) Chinese coin

Gauge

14 hdc x 8 rows = 4" (10 cm)

Design Notes

- This bag uses vintage wool that I picked up at a thrift store and is no longer commercially available through yarn shops. If you can't find this exact yarn, see the substitution suggestion in the variations below. Vintage wool can be found in thrift stores, on auction sites, and at some yarn stores.

- Baste the opening of the bag first, then baste the flap to the front of the bag to keep the unattached edges from stretching out of shape during felting.

- The leather strap was recycled from a bag I found at a thrift store. I used a seam ripper to remove the stitches that held the ends of the strap to the sides of the bag, then sewed the ends to the felted bag with a needle and doubled thread using the perforated holes as a guide.

- Follow the manufacturer's directions on the back of the package for instructions on placing grommets (or see my tips for setting grommets on page 117).

Stitch Guide

Hdc-flo: Half double crochet through front loop only.

Instructions

Follow the instructions for making The Tube Bag (page 57) but do not fasten off. Continue on to make the flap.

FLAP

Ch 2, turn. Hdc-flo in each of next 50 sts across, ch 2, turn. Working in rows, continue in hdc-flo for 9 inches (23 cm) from beginning of flap.

Fasten off and loosely weave in ends.

Finishing

Turn the bag inside out. Thread the wool yarn onto the large-eye yarn needle and whipstitch (see page 48) one end of the tube together to form the bottom. Make sure the flap spans the width of the back. Fold the bottom corner points in 1 inch (2.5 cm) with the tip of the points aligned with the seam and work a couple of stitches to secure (see photo on page 58). Turn the bag right side out. With the scrap of cotton yarn, loosely baste (see page 49) the opening of the bag together, then baste the flap to the front with the edges aligned with the sides of the bag.

Follow the instructions on page 44 for felting in the washing machine. Once the bag has felted to size, roll it in a towel to remove the excess water and then remove the basting stitches. Insert the form; make sure it fits snugly. Pull the edges of the flap to reshape if necessary, then pin the flap to the bag, making sure the edges line up evenly with the sides of the bag. Set in a warm place and allow the bag to dry completely (this may take up to a couple of days).

HANDLES

Once the bag has dried, sew the strap tabs to the sides of the bag using the sewing needle and matching doubled thread.

GROMMETS

Using the knitting needle, make four holes evenly spaced up the center of the flap. Trim the holes to the size of the grommet center and attach the grommets per the manufacturer's directions. Fold the leather lacing in half. Make an overhand knot 1 inch (2.5 cm) from the folded end to form a loop. Beginning with the grommet closest to the bottom edge of the flap, thread both tail ends of the lacing from front to back, then weave in and out of the grommets. Bring the lacing around the back of the bag and up to the front. Thread the tail ends through the Chinese coin. Pull the coin through the loop and make an overhand knot with the long laces to keep the coin from sliding off.

Variations

Try some simple embroidery to embellish the Hong Kong Bag. The tree trunk is outlined with split stitches and several autumnal colors for the leaves were made with French knots (see page 153). I ended up giving this bag to my mom for her birthday, but she was kind enough to allow me to include a photo of it here.

To substitute the yarn, use 450 yards (411 m) of 100 percent animal fiber in worsted weight; do not use superwash.

FLOWeR BasKeT BaG

Brighten up gray days with this little flowering felted bag. A simple adaptation of the felted tube bag, this pattern uses a few shaping stitches so the bag grows wider as you stitch. "Draw" a flower on the front of the bag using a long, felted chain and you're set.

Finished Size

BAG

Before felting: 14" bottom and 19" top (w) x 13" (h) [35.5 and 48 cm x 33 cm]

After felting: 10" bottom and 14" top (w) x 9" (h) [25.5 and 35.5 cm x 23 cm]

HANDLES

Before felting: 80" (w) x 2" (h) [203 cm x 5 cm], before seaming

After felting: 56" (w) x 1/2" (h) [142 cm x 1 cm]

Materials

Cascade 220 (100% Peruvian wool; 220 yards [201 m]; 3.5 ounces [100g]; CYCA #4 worsted)

- 1 skein #2403 brown (MC)
- 1 skein #8913 pink (CC)
- 1 skein #2427 burgundy (CC2)

Size 5.5 mm (I/9) hook

Large-eye yarn needle

Pins

Knitting needle or screwdriver

Small scissors

Gauge

14 hdc x 9 rows = 4" (10 cm)

Design Notes

- Don't bother to baste the opening closed on this one. The idea is to have a flared open edge, so it's fine if it stretches a bit in the wash.

Stitch Guide

Increase: Work 2 hdc-flo in the same stitch.

Couching: The flower design is attached to the bag using a simple embroidery stitch called couching. Couching is used to attach fibers that are too thick to pass through a fabric. With yarn (or thread) threaded onto the needle and the fabric facing you, bring the needle from back to front, over the felted chain (or any thick fiber) and back through the fabric on the other side. Move up 1/4 to 1/2 inch (0.3 to 0.5 cm) and make another stitch.

Instructions

BAG

Follow the instructions for The Tube Bag (page 57) but add one increase in every other round. Place your increases randomly in the round, being sure not to stack them right on top of each other. To make the colorblock stripe, begin with MC and work for 9 inches (23 cm), then switch to CC for the remaining 3 inches (7.5 cm). Fasten off and loosely weave in ends.

HANDLES

With CC2, ch 280.

Row 1: Hdc in 2nd ch from hook and in each ch across, turn.

Rows 2–5: Ch 2, hdc in each st across, turn.

Fold the piece in half so you are seaming the long edges together and loosely sl st through both layers. Fasten off and weave in loose ends.

Holding two strands of CC2, ch 50. Fasten off.

Finishing

Turn the bag inside out. Thread the wool yarn onto the large-eye yarn needle and whipstitch (see page 48) the shorter end of the tube together to form the bottom. Fold the bottom corner points in 1 inch (2.5 cm), with the tip of the point aligned with the seam, and work a couple of stitches to secure (see photo on page 58). Turn the bag right side out.

Place the bag, handle, and motif cord in a laundry bag or pillowcase and follow the instructions on page 44 for felting in the washing machine. Once the pieces have felted to size, roll each one in a towel to remove the excess water. Shape the bag, flaring out the top edge, and pin it to a folded towel so it retains its shape as it dries. Cut the handle into two equal pieces and hand-felt the cut ends by scrubbing them with hot water and a small amount of soap. Set the pieces in a warm place to dry completely (this may take up to a couple of days).

Once the pieces are dry, use the knitting needle to make two holes for the handles on each side of the bag about 2 inches (5 cm) from the top edge and equally spaced from the sides. Using the small scissors, snip the opening wide enough to slide one end of the strap through. If you feel that the fabric at the openings needs a little smoothing out, scrub the raw edges with hot, soapy water until the stitches become invisible. Thread each end of the handles into the holes from the inside out and make an overhand knot close to each end.

Shape the felted cord into a flower design on the front of the bag. Pin the design in place to keep it from moving while you work. Couch the design to the bag (see photo at right) using the same color yarn and the large-eye yarn needle. Finish by placing a stitch through the tail end of the cord and weave in any ends on the wrong side of the bag.

Variations

To substitute the yarns, use 440 yards [400 m] total (220 yards [200 m] of MC, 110 yards [100 m] each of CC and CC2) of 100 percent animal fiber in a worsted weight; do not use superwash.

Instead of using the colorblock shown, make this bag all in one color.

Make the top edge even wider by adding more increases. Increase every other round by two stitches or work one increase on each round.

THE WINDOW BAG

Crochet, felt, and cut. The idea for this bag began with the cutout handles, but once I started cutting, I didn't want to stop. Next I made little windows that look into a fabric garden. This process of layering any felted fabric on top of another fabric is a loose interpretation of a quilting method known as reverse appliqué. The result is stylish in a retro, mod, and handcrafted way.

Finished Size

Before felting: 15" (w) x 18" (h) [38 cm x 46 cm]

After felting: 11" (w) x 12¹/₂" (h) [28 cm x 32 cm]

Materials

3 skeins Cascade Pastaza (50% llama, 50% wool; 132 yards [120 m]; 3.5 ounces [100 g]; CYCA #4 worsted) in #84 blue

Size 5.5 mm (I/9) hook

Stitch marker

Large-eye yarn needle

Pins

Small scissors

Paper, for circle templates

Chalk, for tracing

10 yards (9 m) Papermart Wraffia Ribbon in #45 terra cotta

³/₄ yard (0.7 m) lining fabric in orange floral pattern

Sewing needle

Thread to match the lining fabric

Gauge

13 hdc x 8 rows = 4" (10 cm)

Design Notes

- To help keep track of rounds during the decrease portion of the pattern, place a stitch marker in the first stitch of the round. Move the marker up with each round.

- You can cut any shapes you want from your felted fabric; however, the smaller the piece, the more basic your shapes should be. Large and complicated shapes work best on large felted surfaces like rugs. To experiment with the shapes you have in mind, try them out on a felted swatch before you cut your bag.

Stitch Guide

Hdc-flo: Half double crochet through front loop only.

Hdc-flo2tog: Half double crochet two sts together using the front loop only. Yo, insert hook in front loop of next st, yo and draw up loop, insert hook in front loop of next st, yo and draw up loop, yo and draw through all 4 sts on hook.

Blanket Stitch: The blanket stitch, aka the buttonhole stitch, is a decorative embroidery stitch commonly used as an edging. With the front of the piece facing you, hold the tail end on the back side to secure and bring the needle from back to front through the opening. Insert the needle from front to back at the guideline. Bring the point of the needle back through the opening in front of the loop of fiber along the edge of the opening, and pull the needle all the way through to complete one stitch. Insert the needle ¹/₄ to ¹/₂ inch (0.5 to 1 cm) to the right along the guideline. Bring the point of the needle back through the opening in front of the loop of fiber along the edge of the opening, and pull the needle all the way through to complete the next stitch. Continue working in blanket stitch around. To finish, thread the needle through the first stitch and weave in the ends on the wrong side of the fabric.

Instructions

Follow the instructions for The Tube Bag (page 57) but do not fasten off. Continue on to shape the top for the handles.

BEGIN SHAPING

Row 1: Hdc-flo in next st, [hdc-flo2tog, hdc-flo in each of next 31 sts] three times – 97 hdc.

Row 2: Hdc-flo in each of next 16 sts, [hdc-flo2tog, hdc-flo in each of next 30 sts] twice, hdc-flo2tog, hdc-flo in each of next 15 sts – 94 hdc.

Row 3: Hdc-flo in next st, [hdc-flo2tog, hdc-flo in each of next 29 sts] three times – 91 hdc.

Row 4: Hdc-flo in each of next 15 sts, [hdc-flo2tog, hdc-flo in each of next 28 sts] twice, hdc-flo2tog, hdc-flo in each of next 14 sts – 88 hdc.

Row 5: Hdc-flo in next st, [hdc-flo2tog, hdc-flo in each of next 27 sts] three times – 85 hdc.

Row 6: Hdc-flo in each of next 14 sts, [hdc-flo2tog, hdc-flo in each of next 26 sts] twice, hdc-flo2tog, hdc-flo in each of next 13 sts – 82 hdc.

Row 7: Hdc-flo in each of next 2 sts, [hdc-flo2tog, hdc-flo in each of next 11 sts] six times, hdc-flo in each of next 2 sts – 76 hdc.

Row 8: Hdc-flo in each of next 8 sts, [hdc-flo2tog, hdc-flo in each of next 10 sts] five times, hdc-flo2tog, hdc-flo in each of next 6 sts – 70 hdc.

Row 9: Hdc-flo in each of next 2 sts, [hdc-flo2tog, hdc-flo in each of next 9 sts] six times, hdc-flo in each of next 2 sts – 64 hdc.

Row 10: Hdc-flo in each of next 7 sts, [hdc-flo2tog, hdc-flo in each of next 8 sts] five times, hdc-flo2tog, hdc-flo in each of next 5 sts – 58 hdc.

Row 11: Hdc-flo in each of next 2 sts, [hdc-flo2tog, hdc-flo in each of next 7 sts] six times, hdc-flo in each of next 2 sts – 52 hdc.

Row 12: Hdc-flo in each of next 6 sts, [hdc-flo2tog, hdc-flo in each of next 6 sts] five times, hdc-flo2tog, hdc-flo in each of next 4 sts – 46 hdc.

Row 13: Hdc-flo in each of next 2 sts, [hdc-flo2tog, hdc-flo in each of next 5 sts] six times, hdc-flo in each of next 2 sts – 40 hdc.

Row 14: Hdc-flo in next 5 sts, [hdc-flo2tog, hdc-flo in each of next 4 sts] five times, hdc-flo2tog, hdc-flo in each of next 3 sts – 34 hdc.

Fasten off and loosely weave in ends.

Finishing

Turn the bag inside out. Thread the wool yarn onto the large-eye yarn needle and whipstitch (see page 48) the widest end of the tube together to form the bottom. Turn the bag right side out.

Follow the instructions on page 44 for felting in the washing machine. Once the bag has felted to size, roll it in a towel to remove the excess water. Hand shape the bag, set it in a warm place, and allow it to dry completely (this may take up to a couple of days).

HANDLES

Once the bag has dried, use the scissors to cut a 2-inch-wide (5 cm) oval for the handle. The top of the oval should be centered about 2 inches (5 cm) from the top edge. Cut a slit 3½ inches (9 cm) long along each side of the opening at the top to separate the handles (see photo on page 67).

CUTOUTS

Cut three circles out of paper to use as templates. The circles shown are 2 inches (5 cm), 1½ inches (3.5 cm), and ¾ inch (2 cm) in diameter. Choose whatever size circles you want as long as they are no bigger than 2 inches (5 cm) in diameter. Pin the templates to the bag in your desired locations, then trace around them with chalk. Using the scissors, cut out the circles. If necessary, hand felt the cut edges by scrubbing them with hot, soapy water until the stitches become invisible.

Using the chalk, draw a guideline ½ inch (1 cm) around each cutout. With the Wraffia threaded onto the large-eye yarn needle, blanket stitch around each of the openings. Weave in the ends on the wrong side.

LINING

The lining will need to be doubled because it will be seen from both the inside and the outside through the cutouts.

Cut two 11 inch (28 cm) by 18 inch (46 cm) pieces of lining fabric. Working with one piece at a time, fold the fabric in half with the right sides together to make an 11 inch (28 cm) by 9 inch (23 cm) piece. With the folded edge at the bottom, sew the two sides together with a ½-inch (1 cm) seam allowance, leaving the top edge open. Repeat for the second lining.

Turn one lining right side out and insert it into the second lining. The right side of each lining should face each other. Sew the linings together ¼ inch (0.5 cm) from the top edge, but leave a gap of several inches open at the end. Fasten off.

Reach through the gap and carefully ease out the inside bag (see photo bottom left). Push the inner lining into the outer lining. To close the gap, push the seam allowance inward and pin or press with an iron (see photo bottom right).

Insert the double lining into the bag and pin the top edge to the bag under the cutout handles. With needle and thread, sew the lining to the bag ¼ inch (0.5 cm) from the top edge of the lining with ¼-inch (0.5 cm) backstitches (see page 47). Tack down the bottom corners of the lining to the bottom of the bag with a few stitches to secure.

Variations

To substitute the yarn, use 400 yards (366 m) of 100 percent animal fiber in a worsted weight; do not use superwash. To substitute the raffia, use 10 yards (9 m) of coordinating fiber to stitch around the cut edges.

JUTE FILET BAG

Large-mesh fabrics provide the perfect window for bold, colored linings. The rawness of the jute fiber in this bag complements the bright, modern lining and sleek wooden handles. It's versatile in size, easy to make, and can be completed in just a few hours. The lining makes this a perfectly casual day bag or totable craft bag. Leave the lining off and you can take it to the market to load up with fresh bread and veggies.

Finished Size

12" (w) x 15" (h) [30.5 cm x 38 cm], not including handles

Materials

400 feet (122 m) heavy-duty, three-ply jute twine in natural

Size 6.5 mm (K/10 1/2) hook

1/2 yard (0.5 m) reversible cotton lining fabric in tangerine

Chalk

Scissors

Sewing needle and thread to match lining

1 set Tall Poppy Craft Long sew-on wooden handles (9 1/2" x 2 1/4" [24 cm x 5.5 cm]) in rosewood

Drill with 1/8-inch (3 mm) bit (optional; see Design Notes)

Small-eye yarn needle

Gauge

2 mesh x 4 rows = 4" (10 cm)

Design Notes

- The mesh pattern is worked in joined rounds but with a nifty little joining stitch. Instead of working a slip stitch to join the rounds, work part of the last mesh space (1 chain), then join the round with a double crochet. This little trick sets up the first stitch for the next round, right in the center of the mesh space, creating a virtually invisible seam.

- Do not turn at the end of the round.

- Because of the thickness of the jute fiber, I used a drill to make the holes in the handle a little larger. If you don't have a drill or simply don't want to bother making the holes larger, sew the handles to the bag using a sewing needle and a doubled length of cotton thread.

Stitch Guide

Fsc (Foundation Single Crochet): Ch 2, insert hook in second ch, yo, draw up a loop, ch 1 through first loop on hook, yo, draw through both loops. For second and following fsc, insert hook in ch (found at base of previous fsc), yo, draw up a loop, ch 1 through first loop on hook, yo, draw through both loops.

Instructions

Fsc 56, sl st in first fsc to join, taking care not to twist chain.

Rnds 1–3: Ch 1 (does not count as sc), sc in each st around, sl st in first sc to join – 56 sc.

Rnd 4: Ch 7 (counts as dc and ch 4), *sk next 3 sts, dc in next st, ch 4; rep from * around ending last mesh with ch 1, dc in 3rd ch of beg ch-7 to join – 14 mesh spaces.

> **TIP:** Notice how we joined the round with a double crochet into the beginning chain? Sometimes when you're working in rounds and you want to end in the middle of a space, like a chain space, you can work one of the basic stitches to replace the chains. For example, if you are working a ch-3 space and you want to be in the middle of the next ch-3 space to begin the next round, simply work one chain and a double crochet in the first stitch. Play with stitches and chains to see what looks right for your mesh or lace.

Rnds 5–12: Ch 7 (counts as dc and ch 4), *dc in next ch-4 sp, ch 4; rep from * around ending last mesh with ch 1, dc in 3rd ch of beg ch-7 to join.

Rnd 13: Ch 1, 3 sc in same ch-4 sp, work 4 sc in each ch-4 sp around ending with 1 sc in first ch-4 sp, sl st in first sc to join – 56 sc.

Rnds 14–16: Ch 1 (does not count as sc), sc in each st around, sl st in first sc to join.

Fasten off.

Finishing

Turn the bag inside out. Holding the edges of one end of the tube together, join the jute in the first st through both layers with a sl st. Ch 1 and sl st through both layers of each st across to close the bottom of the bag. Fasten off and weave in loose ends. Turn the bag RS out.

Wet block (see page 45) to finished measurements.

LINING

Fold the fabric in half with RS together and lay it on a flat surface. Lay the bag on top of the fabric with the folded edge at the bottom. Trace around the three sides of the bag with chalk, adding an extra 1/2 inch (1 cm) for the seam allowance and leaving the folded edge intact. Cut along the chalk lines.

With RS together and the folded edge at the bottom, sew the sides together with a 1/2-inch (1 cm) seam allowance, leaving the top open. Turn right side out and insert the lining into the bag. Fold the top edge of the lining 1/4 inch (0.5 cm) to the back. With the raw edge hidden by the band of sc sts at the top of the bag, hand-stitch the lining to the bag about 1/4 inch (0.5 cm) from the top edge. Tack down the bottom corners of the lining to the bottom of the bag with a few sts to secure.

HANDLES

If you need to widen the holes on the handle to accommodate the jute twine, drill through every other hole on the handle. Attach the handles with the small-eye yarn needle and jute using a simple running stitch (see page 49) and weave in any loose ends.

Variations

The mesh pattern works in multiples of four sts. To make the bag wider or narrower, simply add or remove 4 chains for every 1 mesh sp, which is equal to about 2 inches (5 cm) in width.

You can use any sturdy fiber for this bag. Cotton or other plant fibers will help the bag retain its durability and structure. Wool or synthetic fibers will require you to carry a strand of matching cotton thread to reduce the inherent stretch of the fiber. Remember that you may need to adjust your hook size when working with thicker or thinner fibers; always check your gauge before you begin.

vintage satchel

Mixing fabrics and textures is what this project is all about. The strap of almost any bag bears a good portion of the weight from its contents. I wanted to see what kind of crocheted fabric could take on the strain of a heavy bag and found that felted straps stand up to the job. The only problem with felting is that you lose the texture and lace that make crocheted fabric so pretty. So, I mixed it up: this bag has a felted strap, textured crocheted panels, a lacy flap, and some fun strips of patterned fabric.

Finished Size

12" (w) x 13" (h) [30.5 cm x 33 cm], excluding strap

Materials

4 skeins Lily Sugar 'n Cream (100% cotton; 120 yards [109 m]; 2.5 ounces [70 g]; CYCA #4 worsted) in #4 ecru (MC)

1 skein Cascade 220 (100% Peruvian highland wool; 220 yards [200 m]; 3.5 ounces [100 g]; CYCA #4 worsted) in #2403 brown (CC)

Size 5.5 mm (I/9) hook

Sewing needle and thread

Size 5.0 mm (H/8) hook

Large-eye yarn needle

4 x 13-inch (10 x 33 cm) scrap fabric in solid brown

2 1/2 x 13-inch (6.5 x 33 cm) scrap fabric in brown-and-white pattern

Light fusible web

1 skein DMC Six Strand embroidery floss in #608 bright orange

Embroidery needle

Pins

Stitch markers

1/2 yard [0.5 m] cotton lining fabric in cream with brown and red polka dots

Chalk, for tracing

Gauge

11 sts x 9 1/2 rows = 4" (10 cm) with 5.5 mm hook in hdc-flo

14 sts x 14 rows = 4" (10 cm) with 5.0 mm hook in alternating stitch pattern

Design Notes

- The long edges of the strap are finished off with a row of sc in a worsted or thick cotton yarn before felting. After the strap has been felted, snip and remove the cotton edging.

  This leaves holes in the fabric that are big enough to insert a hook, which makes joining the front panels quick and easy.

- The alternating stitch pattern uses a loop of yarn that runs horizontally across the front of the half double crochet stitch from the previous row to create a unique rib of chain stitches down the front of the fabric.

- E-stitches (extended stitches) are regular stitches like the single crochet or double crochet with one additional step to create a slightly taller version of the same stitch. These stitches are taller than the basic stitch but not as tall as the next stitch in line. When working a series of graduating stitches combined with their E-stitch, you create a smooth, sloping curve.

- The turning chain does not count as a stitch throughout this pattern

Stitch Guide

Fhdc (foundation half double crochet): Ch 2, yo, insert hook in second ch from hook, yo, draw up a loop, loosely ch 1 through first loop on hook, yo, draw through all three loops on hook. For second and following fhdc, insert hook in ch (found at the base of the previous fhdc), yo, draw up a loop, loosely ch 1, yo, draw through all three loops on hook.

Hdc-flo: Half double crochet through the front loop only.

Fsc (foundation single crochet): Ch 2, insert hook in second ch from hook, yo, draw up a loop, ch 1 through first loop on hook, yo, draw through both loops. For second and following fsc, insert hook in ch (found at base of previous fsc), yo, draw up a loop, ch 1, yo, draw through both loops.

Sc-fml: Single crochet through the front-most loop of the hdc from the previous row. The front-most loop is found on the front of the st, just below the standard front loop.

Hdc2tog (modified): Insert hook in first st, yo and draw up a loop (2 loops on hook), yo, insert hook in next st, yo and draw up a loop (4 loops on hook), yo and draw through all loops on hook.

Esc: Insert hook in st, yo and draw up a loop, yo and pull through *first* loop on hook, yo and pull through both loops on hook.

Edc: Yo, insert hook in st, yo and draw up a loop, yo and pull through *first* loop on hook, [yo and pull through first 2 loops on hook] twice.

Etr: Yo twice, insert hook in st, yo and draw up a loop, yo and pull through *first* loop on hook, [yo and pull through first 2 loops on hook] three times.

Dtr: Yo three times, insert hook in st, yo and draw up a loop, [yo and pull through first 2 loops on hook] four times.

Edtr: Yo three times, insert hook in st, yo and draw up a loop, yo and pull through *first* loop on hook, [yo and pull through first 2 loops on hook] four times.

Alternating stitch pattern (any number of sts)

Row 1: Ch 1 (does not count as st), hdc in each st across, turn.

Row 2: Ch 1, sc-fml in each stitch across, turn.

Instructions

STRAP/GUSSET

With CC and larger hook, fhdc 295, join with sl st in first fhdc to form ring, taking care not to twist ch.

Rnds 1–8: Ch 1, hdc-flo in each st around, sl st in first hdc to join. Fasten off.

With MC, join yarn with a sl st in any st on one side of the strap, ch 1 and loosely sc in each st around. Fasten off. Rep for second side. Fold the strap in half twice widthwise, then loosely baste the edges together to keep the strap from stretching in the wash. It is not necessary to weave in ends.

Follow the instructions on page 44 for felting in the washing machine. When the strap has felted to the desired texture, roll it in a towel to remove any excess water. Cut and remove the basting sts, then stretch and shape the strap with gentle tugs to work out any uneven edges. Set in a warm place to dry completely. Remove the cotton crochet sts.

FRONT

With smaller hook, fsc 44.

Row 1 (RS): Ch 1, hdc in 2nd ch from hook and in each ch across, turn – 44 hdc.

Row 2: Ch 1, sc-fml in each st across, turn.

Rows 3–38: Rep Rows 1 and 2.

EDGING

With RS facing, work one round of sc evenly around the entire piece to create a border. Work three sc in each corner st, and on edges where you work into the row ends, simply work one sc in each row end, making the edge even and smooth. Sl st in first sc of border to join.

Fasten off and weave in loose ends.

BACK

With smaller hook, fsc 60.

Row 1 (RS): Ch 1, hdc in each st across, turn – 60 hdc.

Row 2: Ch 1, sc-fml in each st across, turn.

Rows 3–14: Rep Rows 1 and 2.

BEGIN SHAPING FLAP

Row 1 (RS): Ch 1, hdc2tog over first 2 sts, hdc in each st across, turn – 59 hdc.

Row 2: Ch 1, sc-fml in each st across, turn.

Rows 3–20: Repeat Rows 1 and 2.

Work evenly in alternating stitch pattern without decreasing for four rows.

EDGING

With RS facing, work one rnd of sc evenly around entire piece to create a border. Work three sc in each corner st, and on edges where you work into the row ends, simply work one sc in each row end, making the edge even and smooth. Sl st in first sc of border to join and turn to work Flap Edge.

FLAP EDGE

The last row is a decorative edge for the bottom of the flap. A series of sts, gradually increasing in height, helps accentuate the curved shaping along the edge of the flap.

With WS facing, ch 1, sc in each of first 5 sts, esc in each of next 3 sts, dc in each of next 3 sts, edc in each of next 3 sts, tr in each of next 3 sts, etr in each of next 3 sts, dtr in each of next 3 sts, edtr in each st to the end of the flap edge.

Fasten off and weave in loose ends with large-eye yarn needle.

FABRIC STRIPS

With RS together, sew one long edge of the fabric scraps together with a 1/2-inch (1 cm) seam allowance to create a fabric panel. Press open the seam. Cut the fusible web to fit the fabric panel, then trim an additional 1/2 inch (1 cm) off all sides so the web is slightly smaller than the fabric. With the paper side up, center the web on the WS of the fabric panel and iron, leaving a 1/2-inch (1 cm) border of fabric on all sides.

Finishing

FRONT

Remove the paper backing from the fusible web on the fabric panel. Fold all four edges of the fabric over to the WS and finger press along the folded edge. Place the fabric panel in the desired location on the front panel and iron in place. With embroidery floss threaded onto a needle, sew the fabric 1/4 inch (0.5 cm) from the edge to the front using a 1/4-inch (0.5 cm) running stitch (see page 49).

Pin the front panel to the felted gusset around three sides with WS together, leaving the top edge unattached for the opening. With smaller hook and RS facing, sc the front panel to the gusset, working under two threads of the crocheted panel and through the holes in the strap. Sc evenly around the three sides of the bag, working 3 sc in each corner, then continue in sc around remaining edge of strap only, sl st in beginning st, turn.

Next round: Ch 1, sl st in each st around. Fasten off.

BACK

First you need to figure out where the back panel becomes the flap. The shaped edge of the back is the flap edge, the straight edge on the opposite side is the bottom edge. Beg at the bottom corner, count 44 stitches up each side, and place a marker. The remainder of the back panel, above the markers, is considered the flap and will not be attached to the gusset.

Pin the back panel to the gusset using the stitch markers and front panel as a guide, leaving the flap unattached. Before joining, make sure the back and front panels are even. Join back panel to gusset same as for front. Fasten off and weave in loose ends.

LINING

Fold the lining fabric in half with RS together. Tuck the flap into the bag so the top edge is flush with the front panel, then lay it on top of the fabric, leaving about 2 inches (5 cm) of the folded fabric edge extending at the bottom. With chalk, trace a line 2 inches (5 cm) from either side of the bag and 1/2 inch (1 cm) from the top edge of the bag. Leaving the folded edge intact, cut along the trace lines. With RS together, sew the sides of the lining together using a 1/2-inch (1 cm) seam allowance. Insert the lining into the bag and pull out the bag flap. Fold the top edge of the lining down 1/2 inch (1 cm) to the WS and pin in place around the opening of the bag. With needle and thread, use 1/8-inch (0.3 cm) backstitches (see page 47) to sew the top edge of the lining to the bag.

Variations

To substitute the yarns, use 400 yards (365 m) of 100 percent cotton in worsted weight (MC) and 250 yards (230 m) of 100 percent animal fiber in worsted weight (CC); do not use superwash.

Because the front and back panels are worked from side to side, adjusting the number of rows you make will make the bag wider or narrower.

If you don't like the length of the finished strap, you can adjust it. Before crocheting the front and back panels to the strap, pin everything together and try it on for size. If the strap is too long, determine how much you need to remove and cut out a section where the strap hits the shoulder. Whipstitch (see page 48) or sew the short ends together. Hand felt the seam by scrubbing with hot water and a little soap until the sts have blended into the rest of the fabric.

patchwork handbag

Quilting was my obsession *du jour* when I came up with the patchwork theme for this bag. The concept is simple, yet it opens itself up to all kinds of creative interpretation based on the textures, fibers, and patterns used in the squares. This bag demonstrates how crochet can be used as a piece of fabric to enhance or embellish a project that uses other materials. A *fat quarter* is a standard sized, 18 x 22-inch (45.5 x 56 cm) piece of fabric often sold for quilting projects (you get four fat quarters when you cut a yard of fabric into quarters). Craft and fabric shops often sell precut fat quarters, which means you don't have to buy more than you need.

Finished Size

10 1/2" (26.5 cm) square, excluding handle

Materials

1 ball Hemp Basics 20-pound hemp twine (100% hemp; 400 feet [121 m]; 3.5 ounces [100 g]) in natural

Size 3.75 mm (F/5) hook

5 cotton fabric fat quarters (18" x 22" [45.5 cm x 56 cm]) in brown floral, white with brown circles, pink floral, burgundy, and a neutral shade (for fusing)

Light fusible web

1/2 yard (45.5 cm) polyester lining fabric in gold

Chalk, for tracing

Sewing needle

Sewing thread in cream, rose pink, burgundy, brown, and gold, or threads to match the fabrics and lining

Pins

1 set Tall Poppy Craft Long with Toggle wooden handles (10" x 2 1/2" [25.5 cm x 6.5 cm]) in cherrywood

6 (7/8-inch [2 cm]) buttons in three colors to coordinate with fabrics

Gauge

18 sc x 16 rows = 4" (10 cm)

Design Notes

- The turning chain does not count as a stitch.

- This is the perfect project to use up scrap fabrics and buttons from your stash.

- The crocheted hemp fabric will be a bit stiff before blocking. Blocking relaxes the fibers, making the square more flexible.

- I machine sewed through both the crocheted hemp and the fabric layers with my trusty old mechanical machine. I'm not sure I would have tried it with my new computerized machine, though. If you are hand sewing the bag, use 1/8- to 1/4-inch (0.3 to 0.5 cm) backstitches (see page 47) for a nice secure seam.

Stitch Guide

Fsc (Foundation Single Crochet): Ch 2, insert hook in second ch from hook, yo, draw up a loop, ch 1 through first loop on hook, yo, draw through both loops. For second and following fsc, insert hook in ch (found at base of previous fsc), yo, draw up a loop, ch 1, yo, draw through both loops.

Flo: Front loop only.

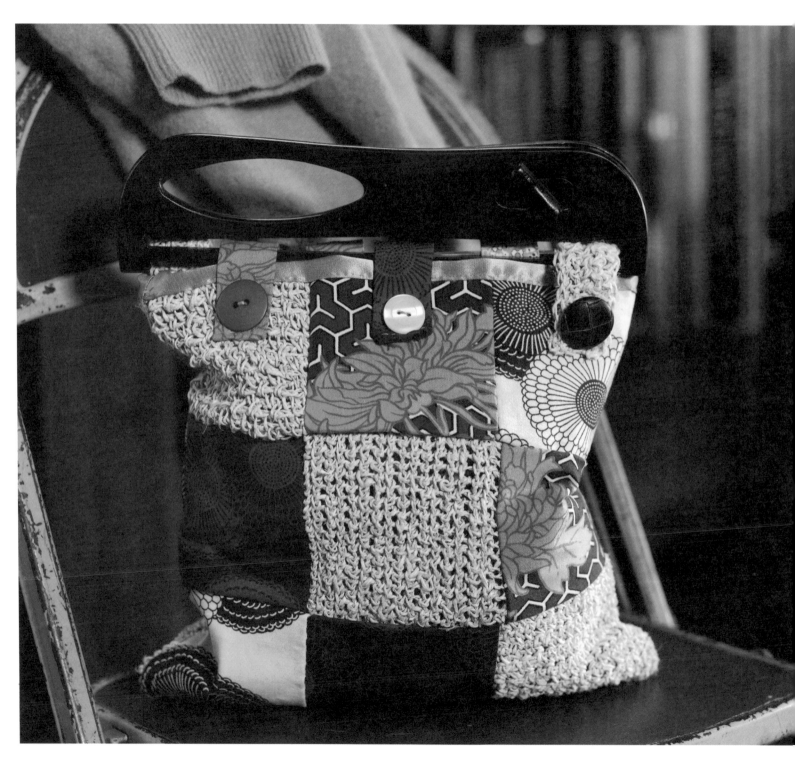

Instructions

BASIC SQUARE (Make 2)

With hemp, fsc 18.

Rows 1–16: Ch 1, sc in each st across, turn.

Fasten off and weave in loose ends.

ALTERNATE BASIC SQUARE (Make 2)

Follow the instructions for the Basic Square above, but work all sts in flo.

WOVEN SQUARE (Make 2)

With hemp, fsc 18.

Row 1: Ch 1, sc in each of first two sts, (ch 1, sk 1 st, sc in next st) across, turn.

Row 2: Ch 1, sc in first st, sc in first ch-1 sp, (ch 1, sk 1 st, sc in next st) across, turn.

Rows 3–15: Rep Row 2 or until desired square size.

Row 16: Ch 1, sc in each st and ch-1 sp across.

Fasten off and weave in loose ends.

FABRIC SQUARES (Make 12)

Set aside the neutral-colored fat quarter that you will be fusing to the back of the squares. Cut one 8-inch (20 cm) square from each of the four fat quarters to be used on the outside of the bag.

Lay the fusible web, paper side up, on top of the fusing fabric. Cut four 8-inch (20 cm) square pieces of fusible web along with the fabric. Working with one square of web and fusing fabric at a time, press with an iron to fuse the layers together. Remove the paper backing from the fusible web and lay one of the

coordinating fabric squares on top. Press with an iron to fuse. Repeat for all squares. Cut four 4-inch (10 cm) squares from each of the 8-inch fused fabric squares, for a total of 12 squares.

CROCHETED TABS (Make 2)

Fsc 20.

Rows 1–4: Ch 1, sc in each st across, turn – 20 sc.

Fasten off and weave in ends.

Finishing

Follow the instructions on page 45 to wet block each crocheted square to 4 inches (10 cm) square.

LINING

Fold the gold lining fabric in half with RS together and place on a flat surface. Lay the bag on top of the fabric with the folded edge at the bottom. Trace around the remaining three sides of

the bag with chalk, adding an extra 1/2 inch (1 cm) for the seam allowance. Cut along the chalk lines, leaving the folded edge intact. With RS together, sew the two sides together, leaving the top open. Do not turn inside out.

PATCHWORK PANEL (Make 2)

Lay out all of the 4-inch (10 cm) squares (hemp and crochet) on a flat surface in 3 rows of 3 squares for the front and the back. Look at the sample in the photograph for guidance or play with the layout of colors and pattern until you reach a desired order.

Working on one panel at a time, sew 3 squares together to form a row and then sew 3 rows together to form a panel as follows: with RS together, pin the first 2 squares of the first row together and sew. Next, sew the third square to the second square to complete the first row. Put down the first row and begin the next row. Continue to sew the squares together, working across in rows until you have 3 rows of 3 squares each. Next sew the 3 rows together, with RS together, to form a 3 x 3 square panel.

Once both panels are made, sew the front panel to the back panel with RS together around the sides and bottom, leaving the top open. Place a damp towel on top of the bag and press with an iron to smooth out and flatten the seams. Turn RS out. Place a damp towel on top of the bag again and press with an iron to smooth out and flatten the outside of the seams.

With the patchwork handbag RS out and the gold lining fabric RS in, insert the patchwork handbag into the lining so the RS are facing each other. Sew the two together 1/2 inch (1 cm) from the top edge, leaving a gap of about 4 inches (10 cm) open at the end. Fasten off. Reach through the gap and gently ease out the patchwork bag and then stuff the lining into the bag. Push the remaining seam allowance of the gap to the WS and pin. Working through both the outside layer of lining and the patchwork panel, sew all the way around the bag 1/4 inch (0.5 cm) from the top.

FABRIC TABS (Make 4)

Now that the bag is assembled, sift through the remaining scraps of fabric to make your tabs. You will need 2 crocheted tabs and 4 fabric tabs. Since the tabs will be centered on one of the top squares of the bag, choose a fabric that will complement, but not match, each square. Once you've settled on the fabrics, cut a 2 1/2 by 5-inch (6.5 by 13 cm) rectangle from each of the four fabrics. With RS facing, fold the fabric in half lengthwise and sew the long edges together with a 1/4-inch (0.5 cm) seam allowance to make a tube. Press the seam open and then turn the tube RS out. Flatten the tube so that the seam is in the center and press with an iron. Fold the short ends over 1/4 inch (0.5 cm) twice to the side with a seam and hem in place using a coordinating thread.

ATTACH HANDLES

Straddle a tab through the handle so one end is centered over one square and the other end is in the same spot on the inside of the bag. Sew along the bottom edge of the tab working through all layers. Sew a button to the front of each tab.

Variations

To substitute the fiber, use 133 yards (122 m) of any double-knit (dk) or light worsted-weight fiber.

The size of this bag is completely adjustable. To change the size of the squares, inc or dec the number of sts in the foundation row to make the width larger or smaller. To adjust the height, simply work in rows until you have a perfect square. Alternatively, you can add more squares to make the bag bigger.

To design your own patchwork theme, simply crochet a few squares using any lightweight fiber. Cut several squares of coordinating fabrics to the same size and play with the design. When mixing up your own fabrics and fibers, try to match them to each other: hemp pairs well with cotton fabrics, and wool or felted fibers are a great match for knit fabrics.

{ 5 }

Design
The Basics of Shaping

The process of design begins with inspiration, the fuel that lights the creative spark. I'm inspired by everything I see, whether it's the pattern on a scrap of fabric (see Random Stripe Tote on page 111), the shape of a bag in a store window (see The Window Bag on page 65), something I have a need for (see Geometric Pincushions on page 119), or a crazy idea that I just want to see if I can pull off (see Sake Set on page 131).

Sometimes a project is created on the fly; I fiddle with a particular fiber, trying out new stitches and shapes until I've found something I like. Sometimes, I plan the whole design before I get started. Either way, I need to have an understanding of the ways crocheted fabric works to make my way from inspiration to design. In the pages that follow, I outline my own process and introduce the basics of shaping crocheted fabric so you can start designing from scratch, too.

SKETCH IT

Once I have an idea, I make a sketch of it so I don't forget what I was thinking before I have a chance to start crocheting. Use whatever you have on hand to make a quick sketch the moment the idea pops into your head, be it scratch paper, an old receipt, or a cocktail napkin. You can flesh out the sketch later with dimensions and color, but for now, the sketch helps you visualize how your idea will be created, from the bottom up, the top down, or from side to side. If you really want to know what your project will look like full scale, make a paper template for each piece and tape it together. You can even use the template as you crochet to double-check the placement of your shaping stitches.

SWATCH IT

With a fully fleshed out sketch, I need to figure out what materials will bring the design to life. Creating a swatch lets you play with stitch patterns and fibers to determine which are most suitable for the project's final purpose. As you learned in the Basics section, swatching is a made-up term to describe the process of working up a sample of fabric in a particular stitch pattern to figure out which tools you need to create the project in your head. You may not get the desired fabric the first time you swatch, but you'll learn something about the fiber that will help you get closer.

Once you've chosen your fiber, make a quick assessment of its thickness. Bulky fibers like sisal bundling twine will require a fairly large hook size (9.0 mm or so). Thin fibers like 1.0 mm hemp twine will require a smaller hook size (try 3.5 mm). You can always change the size of the hook if you don't like the fabric it creates; that's the point of making a swatch (for more information about making swatches, see page 33).

HOW DOES IT DRAPE?

Think about your finished project: Does it need to be strong and stand up on its own? Or is the project more delicate, requiring soft and loose fibers that hang prettily? Once you complete your first swatch, play with it.

Stretch it, fold it, and squish it. Is the fabric loose and fluid or crisp and stiff? Describing the way a fabric hangs (or doesn't) is its drape—and drape is one of the most important things to consider when designing a project from scratch (so your vases don't droop and your cotton washcloths don't scratch).

The primary factors affecting drape are stitch pattern, hook size, and fiber. Chain stitches and tall stitches like double crochet create flexible and fluid fabrics. Dense single crochet stitches will give you stiffness and rigidity (known as a lack of drape). To change the drape of a fabric, change the hook size first. Use a smaller hook size to tighten the stitches and a larger hook size to loosen them.

If changing the hook size alone doesn't work, there are a few other ways to adjust the drape. To make the fabric stiffer:

- Double up on the fiber. By carrying two strands of 1.0 mm fiber, you end up with a 2.0 mm fiber. You can carry more than two strands together, but keep in mind that the more you carry, the more difficult it is to work the fiber. Be sure to adjust the hook size when you carry additional strands. Also, carrying different colors will result in a flecked or tweed appearance, which can be really cool.

- Crochet into the center of the stitch between the vertical threads instead of under the top two loops.

- Crochet over another fiber. Working over a cotton cord like clothesline allows you to create a very firm and textured fabric. You can also crochet over wire. Crocheting over 20- to 22-gauge wire allows you to form the finished project into almost any shape you want.

- Use a fabric stiffener. Fabric stiffener is a tintable gluelike substance used to shape and stiffen most fabrics, including crochet. Use it straight out of the bottle or dilute it with up to 50 percent water, depending on the amount of stiffness desired.

To make the fabric looser:

- Use a taller stitch or a lacier stitch pattern. Working in a solid single crochet stitch pattern will likely result in a firm, tightly knit fabric. Try switching to double crochet or alternate stitches by skipping one stitch and replacing it with a chain stitch. Taller stitch shell patterns (multiple stitches in the same space) and mesh patterns will usually result in a more flexible fabric.

- Use a thinner fiber. Many fibers—like jute, cotton, and hemp—are available in a range of thicknesses from 0.8 mm to 3.0 mm and up. If you're using a 2.0 mm hemp cord, you will definitely improve the drape by switching to a 1.0 mm cord.

- Try blocking the fabric. Blocking (see page 45) can make dramatic improvements in the drape of your fabric, especially if you are using plant and animal fibers.

Gauge

Now that you've sketched, swatched, and decided on the drape and stitch pattern of your new project, you're ready to move on. In the Basics section, I talked about how important it is to match your gauge to a pattern's gauge. Thinking about gauge in your own design is actually a magical thing. Knowing the gauge can help you figure out the whole pattern without even making the first foundation stitch. If you like the way your swatch looks, then use it to figure out your gauge and you've pretty much just written the pattern.

By knowing the number of stitches and rows within each inch, you can calculate the number of foundation stitches you need to start with, how many rows it will take to finish the project, and where you need to put the increases, decreases, buttonholes, or anything else for that matter. Once the swatch is complete, combine the gauge from the swatch and the measurements from the sketch, and voilà, now you can figure out about how many stitches and rows are needed to make your fabulous design. Unfortunately, many of the alternative fibers I use in this book do not come with a handy gauge printed on the label. So if you decide to use these fibers in your own projects, you'll have to figure out the gauge yourself (for more information about gauge, see page 34).

DO I HavE EnoUGH FIBer?

You've selected your fiber, made the perfect swatch, and calculated your gauge. With this information you can figure out how many yards of your chosen fiber are required to complete your project. All you need is your swatch and a measuring tape (or ruler). Make sure you've written down all the information you need from your swatch before you begin to calculate the estimated yardage.

There are two ways to estimate how much fiber you'll need to make a project. In Method 1, you have to know roughly how many stitches will be used to create your project. In Method 2, you have to know the final dimensions of the project. Either way, the calculations are only estimates, so it's always helpful to buy a little more fiber than you think you'll need in case you're off or you have to make adjustments.

TIP: Method 1: You know about how many stitches will be used in the project.

Say you have a swatch with the following dimensions:
20 sts wide x 10 rows deep

And you know that your project will use roughly 4,000 sts.

1. Calculate the number of total sts in your swatch by multiplying the number of sts per row by the number of rows.
20 sts x 10 rows = 200 sts

2. Mark the point where the working yarn comes out of the last st with a slip knot, then unravel the swatch and measure the total number of yards used to create it. **15 yards (14 m)**

3. Divide the total number of sts in the swatch by the total number of yards to get the number of sts per yard.
200 sts ÷ 15 yards = 13.3 sts per yard (1 m)

4. Divide the total number of sts in the project by the number of sts per yard, which equals the number of yards required to create the project. **4,000 sts ÷ 13.3 sts per yard = 301 yards (274 m)**

TIP: Method 2: You know the dimensions of the project.

Say you have a swatch with the following dimensions:
4 inches (10 cm) wide x 4 inches (10 cm) long

The project is a rectangular bag with 12 x 8-inch (30.5 x 20 cm) panels making up the front and back of the bag.

1. Figure out the total number of square inches for the swatch by multiplying the width by the length. **4 x 4 = 16 square inches (40.5 cm)**

2. Figure out the total number of square inches for the project by multiplying the width by the length. This will likely be a rough estimate if the project has multiple angles.
12 x 8 = 96 square inches (244 cm) per panel x 2 for each panel = 192 square inches (488 cm) total

3. Figure out how many times the area of the swatch will fit into the area of the project by dividing the total number of square inches for the project by the total number of square inches for the swatch.
192 sq in for project ÷ 16 sq in for swatch = 12

4. Mark the point where the yarn comes out of the last stitch of the swatch with a slip knot, then unravel and measure the total number of yards used to create it. **20 yards (18.5 m)**

5. Figure out the total number of yards needed for the project by multiplying the number in step 3 by the total number of yards used to create the swatch. **12 x 20 yds = 240 yds (218.5 m)**

SHAPING

Now that you know how much fiber you need, let's talk about the nitty-gritty of design: shaping. Crocheted fabric can easily be sculpted into a variety of shapes, from a flat and square coaster to a three-dimensional vase. Regardless of the details of final construction, most projects start off with a geometric pattern. Figuring out how to create the shape you envision is the next step of designing a project from scratch.

The projects in this chapter address the principles of shaping by showing you how to create several of the most common geometric patterns used in crochet: circles, squares, triangles, ovals, and rectangles. Whether you're working back-and-forth in rows or in rounds, the location and frequency of increases and decreases determines the sharpness of a shape's angles.

For example:

- Working increases or decreases at or close to the beginning or end of the row creates a sharp angle along the edge.

- Working increases or decreases close to the center of the row creates a gradual angle that spikes or bows at the middle and softens at the edge.

- Working increases or decreases on every row makes the fabric take shape quickly, whereas alternating increase or decrease rows with one or more even rows allows the shape to develop more slowly.

- Working a series of stitches that vary in height can create curves, slopes, or sharp angles; for example, I used this technique to create the angle of the flap in the Vintage Satchel (page 73).

These shaping guidelines allow you to create any shape you can imagine—whether simple or complex. Although it might take some trial and error to get the shaping perfect, sometimes the fun is in the process. Each of the projects that follows began with a basic shape. To help you learn more about the possibilities of designing with crochet, I introduce simple techniques for making each shape and include instructions for sample swatches that let you practice—and master—shaping principles. When sample swatching, use whatever yarn or hook you have on hand. For practical swatches, use a 5.0 mm hook and 100 percent cotton yarn, then use your geometric swatches as facecloths.

Art of the Circle

Crocheting circles is a form of meditation: around and around, making striped circles, lacy circles, dense circles, great big circles, and very little circles. Try it and you'll see: circles are relaxing and fun. They can also be addictive. I carry a ball of yarn and a hook in my bag at all times, so I end up crocheting circles while waiting in line at the post office or grocery store and while sitting with my husband at a football game.

So once you have a dozen or so circles spilling from your bag, what do you do with them? Lots of things. You can layer a few circles of varying sizes and colors on top of each other, stitch them together, and top them off with a vintage or hand-crocheted button. I use simple, flowerlike pieces to adorn bags or I add a pin to the back to make a brooch. You could crochet a lacy circle using a bright cotton thread for a modern take on the heirloom doily. You could even make a great big circular area rug out of jute or sisal, although I wouldn't recommend working on this while in line at the store.

To crochet a circle, start from the center and work your way out, increasing stitches with every round to make the circle grow. The number of increases depends on the final desired shape of the circle: flat, concave, or ruffled.

FLAT CIRCLES

To crochet a flat circle, each round needs to be increased by the same number of stitches that were worked in the first round. So, if you started with 6 single crochet stitches in the first round, the next round should have 12 stitches, the following round should have 18 stitches, and so on. The taller the stitch, the faster the circle grows, so you should work a few more stitches in each round. Here is a general rule of thumb when making circles from scratch:

Stitch	Round 1	Increases per Round
Single Crochet	4–6	4–6
Half Double Crochet	7–9	7–9
Double Crochet	10–12	10–12

Flat circles are used to make the Red's Goodie Basket (page 95) and the Corde Market Bag (page 139).

Joining rounds creates a circle with concentric rings (above left) and not joining rounds creates a spiral (above right)

TIP: To create a spiral instead of concentric circles, work a flat circle as described above without joining at the end of each round. Placing a stitch marker in the first stitch of each round will help you keep track of the rounds. Each time you come to the stitch marker, begin a new round and move the marker up to the new first stitch.

SAMPLE FLAT CIRCLE SWATCH

Start with an adjustable ring (see page 38).

Rnd 1: Ch 1 (does not count as sc throughout), work 6 sc into the ring, sl st in first sc to join – 6 sc.

Rnd 2: Ch 1, work 2 sc in each st around, sl st in first sc to join – 12 sc.

Rnd 3: Ch 1, sc in first st, *2 sc in next st, sc in next st; rep from * around ending with 2 sc in last st, sl st in first sc to join – 18 sc.

Rnd 4: Ch 1, 2 sc in first st, *sc in each of next 2 sts, 2 sc in next st; rep from * around ending with sc in each of last 2 sts, sl st in first sc to join – 24 sc.

Rnd 5: Ch 1, sc in each of first 3 sts, *2 sc in next st, sc in each of next 3 sts; rep from * around ending with 2 sc in last st, sl st in first sc to join – 30 sc.

Rnd 6: Ch 1, 2 sc in first st, *sc in each of next 4 sts, 2 sc in next st; rep from * around ending sc in each of last 4 sts, sl st in first sc to join – 36 sc.

Continue to work one more sc st between increases (2 sc in same st) around to increase each rnd by 6 sts until the circle is as big as you'd like it to be.

To create a near perfect circle, you will need to disperse the increases evenly throughout the round and make sure they are not stacked right on top of each other on subsequent rounds. If you consistently work an increase on top of an increase from the previous round you will create a circle with distinctive corners: a hexagon for six increases, an octagon for eight, and so on.

CONCAVE CIRCLES

To create concave circles—perfect for bowls, bags, or vases—increase each round by a smaller number of stitches than you started with in the first round. The fewer the increases in each round, the more quickly the circle will curve inward. Concave circles are used to make The Perfect Bin (page 93) and Red's Goodie Basket (page 95).

CONVEX CIRCLES

To create convex circles—a shape that ruffles or curves outward—increase each round by more stitches than you started with in the first round. The more increases you work in each round, the more quickly the shape will begin to warp and ruffle. Increasing each round by the same number of stitches each time will eventually form exaggerated ruffles and curves that resemble lettuce leaves. Convex shaping is used to make the top edge of Red's Goodie Basket (page 95).

B-Square

Squares can be worked in the round with strategically placed increases that produce a square instead of a circle or a triangle. If you don't want to work in the round, you can also make a square by working the same number of stitches back and forth in rows until the piece is as long as it is wide.

Working squares in rows is easy, but working squares in the round is easy and fun. As with circles, you can start with an adjustable ring. Unlike with circles, you must work the first round of stitches

in a multiple of four: 4, 8, 12, 16, and so on. By working in multiples of four, you can place increase stitches in each of the four corners to make four equally spaced edges. Squares are used to make the Leather Grannies (page 99).

SAMPLE SQUARE SWATCH

Start with an adjustable ring (see page 38).

Rnd 1: Ch 3 (counts as first dc throughout), work 7 dc into the ring, sl st in 3rd ch of beg ch-3 to join – 8 dc.

Rnd 2: Ch 3, *3 dc in next st, dc in next st; rep from * twice, 3 dc in last st, sl st in 3rd ch of beg ch-3 to join – 16 dc.

Rnd 3: Ch 3, dc in next st, *3 dc in next st, dc in each of next 3 sts; rep from * twice, 3 dc in next st, dc in last st, sl st in 3rd ch of beg ch-3 to join – 24 dc.

Rnd 4: Ch 3, dc in each of next 2 sts, *3 dc in next st, dc in each of next 5 sts; rep from * twice, 3 dc in next st, dc in each of last 2 sts, sl st in 3rd ch of beg ch-3 to join – 32 sc.

Rnd 5: Ch 3, dc in each of next 3 sts, *3 dc in next st, dc in each of next 7 sts; rep from * twice, 3 dc in next st, dc in each of last 3 sts, sl st in 3rd ch of beg ch-3 to join – 40 sc.

To continue, work the corner group of 3-dc sts in the center st of the previous corner group until square is of desired size.

TIP: A quick way to see whether your square is actually square is to fold it in half diagonally. If one corner meets the opposite corner and all edges are flush, you've got a square. If the edges aren't flush when the corners meet, add or remove rows until they are. For a more scientific approach, measure the width of your wanna-be square in inches, then figure out the number of rows to 1 inch (2.5 cm). Multiply the number of rows per inch by the width to discover the number of rows you need to make a square.

A Cute Triangle

Like squares, triangles can be worked either back and forth in rows or in the round.

To work a triangle in rows, you can start at the point or the base. To start at the point, make one chain for the first stitch followed by the regular number of turning chains for the type of stitch you plan to work in (see page 20). Work three stitches in the first chain, then continue to add stitches on every row or alternate rows of increases with even rows. The number and frequency of increases will deter-

mine the type of triangle you end up with—equilateral, acute, or isosceles, tall, short, fat, or thin.

To start at the base of the triangle, make the desired number of chains to create the width of the base and then work decreases until you reach the point.

Triangles are used to make the Strappy Clutch (page 107).

SAMPLE TRIANGLE SWATCH BEGINNING AT THE POINT: ISOSCELES TRIANGLE

Ch 2.

Row 1: Work 3 sc in 2nd ch from hook, turn – 3 sc.

Row 2: Ch 1, 2 sc in first st, sc in next st, 2 sc in last st, turn – 5 sc.

Row 3: Ch 1, sc in each st across, turn.

Row 4: Ch 1, 2 sc in first st, sc in each st across to last st, 2 sc in last st, turn.

Rep Rows 3 and 4 for pattern.

In this example, we increase every other row by 2 sts.

SAMPLE TRIANGLE SWATCH BEGINNING AT THE BASE: EQUILATERAL TRIANGLE

Ch 10.

Row 1: Sc in 2nd ch from hook, sc in each st across, turn – 9 sc.

Row 2: Ch 1, sc2tog (decrease) over first 2 sts, sc in each st across, turn – 8 sc.

Rep Row 2 until 3 stitches remain.

Last row: Ch 1, sc3tog over all 3 sts.

To work a triangle in the round, start with a circle. For an equilateral triangle, which has three equal sides, start with a multiple of three stitches in the center ring: 3, 6, 9, and so on, then work three groups of increases equally spaced apart.

Triangles in the round are used to make the Geometric Pincushions (page 119).

Ovals and Rectangles

I've grouped ovals and rectangles together because they are both started with the same first row. You work your first row of stitches across a foundation chain ending with three stitches in the last chain, then you rotate the piece and continue to work across the bottom of the foundation chain, ending with two stitches in the last chain (the same chain you worked the first stitch into).

The first round will have an oval shape with the same number of stitches on top and bottom and a three-stitch group on both ends. To continue the oval shaping, increase each round by six increases, dividing them up by working three increases at each end. To make the

> **TIP:** To figure out how many inches your foundation chain should be to create an oval or a rectangle of a particular size, find the difference between the length and width of the finished size of your shape. For example, a 16 by 10-inch (40.5 by 25.5 cm) rectangle requires a 6-inch (15 cm) foundation chain.

rounded ends more smooth, avoid stacking the increases right on top of each other. Ovals are used to make the Yo-Yo Basket Bag (page 101).

SAMPLE OVAL SWATCH

Ch 13.

Rnd 1: Sc in 2nd ch from hook, sc in each st across to last ch, 3 sc in last ch, rotate work and continue across the bottom of the foundation ch, sc in each st across to last ch, 2 sc in last ch (same ch you worked the first st into), sl st in first sc to join – 26 sc.

Rnd 2: Ch 1 (does not count as st throughout), 2 sc in first st (mark the 2nd st), sc in each st across to 3-sc group, work 2 sc in each st of the 3-sc group (mark the 2nd st of each inc), sc in each st across to 2-sc group, work 2 sc in each st of the 2-sc group (mark the 2nd st of each inc), sl st in first st to join – 32 sc.

Rnd 3: Ch 1, sc in first st, 2 sc in marked st, sc in each st around working 2 sc in each marked st, sl st in first st to join – total inc of 6 sts.

Repeat Rnd 3, working 3 inc at each end of the oval, until desired size.

To make a rectangle, work the first rnd as you would an oval, marking the first and third stitches of the three-stitch group at each end to mark the four corners of the shape. Continue to work in the round working three stitches in the marked stitches at each of the four corners as you would a square. To help you keep track of where to increase, put stitch markers in the center stitch of each corner group. Rectangles are used to make the Random Stripe Tote (page 111) and the Pacific Coast Basket (page 115).

SAMPLE RECTANGLE SWATCH

Ch 13.

Rnd 1: Sc in 2nd ch from hook, sc in each st across to last ch, 3 sc in last ch (mark the first and last st of the 3-sc group), rotate work and continue across the bottom of the foundation ch, sc in each st across to last ch, 2 sc in last ch (mark the first st of this 2-sc group), sl st in first sc to join – 26 sc.

Rnd 2: Ch 1 (does not count as st throughout), 3 sc in first st (mark the 2nd st in the group), sc in each st across to first marker, 3 sc in marked stitch (mark the 2nd st in the group), sc in next st, 3 sc in next marked st (mark the 2nd st in the group), sc in each st across to last marker, 3 sc in marked st (mark the 2nd st in the group), sc in next st, sl st in first st to join – 34 sc.

Rnd 3: Ch 1, sc in each st around, working 3 sc in each marked st and moving the marker up to the 2nd st of the new corner group, sl st in first st to join – total inc of 8 sts.

Repeat Rnd 3 until rectangle is desired size.

My friend Ellen thinks granny squares are the building blocks of fashion. And while I'm not entirely sure about the validity of that statement, the basic shaping principles explored in this chapter are the building blocks of crochet design. Master these techniques in the projects that follow, then in the next chapter, we'll use these building blocks to experiment with fibers and fabrics.

THE PErFECT BIN

This project uses tight, compact stitches and sturdy fiber to create a stiff little container for sewing notions, stitch markers, or jewelry. To make the lid, you just follow the first part of the container pattern and stop when the lid is the size you want. Whether plain or embellished, open or lidded, this quick project can be completed in just an hour or two.

Finished Size

4" (w) x 3" (h) [10 cm x 7.5 cm]

Materials

190 feet (58 m) heavy-duty, three-ply jute twine in natural

Size 5.5 mm (I/9) hook

Size 6.0 mm (J/10) hook

Large-eye yarn needle

Recycled and felted red Fair Isle sweater; see Variations for substitutions

Sewing needle

Sewing thread in orange

1 (1-inch [2.5 cm]) four-holed button in marbled cream

1 ($1/2$-inch [1.3 cm]) four-holed button in red

Gauge

10 sc x 10 rows = 4" (10 cm) with smaller hook

Design Notes

- The pattern begins with a series of increase rounds to make the base. Once the base is the desired width, work a turning round in the back loop only to create a crisp edge, then work a few even rounds until the container is the desired height.

- Tight, compact stitches are necessary to make the container stand up on its own. Adjust the hook size to make your stitches as tight as possible without hurting your hands.

- The bottom of the container is worked in joined rounds but not turned at the end of the round. After you turn to work the body, the pattern is worked in a spiral without joining ends.

- The turning chain does not count as a stitch.

- Follow the instructions on page 44 to felt the recycled sweater.

Stitch Guide

Sc-blo: Single crochet through the back loop of the stitch.

Instructions

Using the jute and the smaller hook, make an adjustable ring (see page 38).

Rnd 1: Work 6 sc in ring, sl st in first sc to join, do not turn.

Rnd 2: 2 sc in each st around, sl st in first sc to join – 12 sc.

Rnd 3: Ch 1, sc in first st, 2 sc in next st, *sc in next st, 2 sc in next st; rep from * around, sl st in first sc to join – 18 sc.

Rnd 4: Ch 1, 2 sc in first st, sc in each of next 2 sts, *2 sc in next st, sc in each of next 2 sts; rep from * around, sl st to first sc in join – 24 sc.

Rnd 5: Ch 1, sc in each of first 3 sts, 2 sc in next st, *sc in each of next 3 sts, 2 sc in next st; rep from * around, sl st in first sc to join – 30 sc.

Rnd 6 (turning round): Sc-blo in each st around.

Rnds 7–10 (even rounds): Sc in each st around.

Fasten off and weave in loose ends with a large-eye needle.

LID

Using the larger hook, follow the patt for the base of the container through Rnd 5. **Next round:** Ch 1, 2 sc in first st, sc in each of next 4 sts, *2 sc in next st, sc in each of next 4 sts; rep from * around, sl st to first sc in join – 36 sc.

Work rnds 6–7 of Base. Fasten off and weave in loose ends.

Finishing

Trace or photocopy the templates at 100 percent and cut out the shapes. Using the paper templates as a guide, cut 12 large petals and 2 circles from a solid colored piece of the felted sweater. Cut 5 small petals from a Fair Isle piece (this is the pattern usually found along the chest) of the felted sweater.

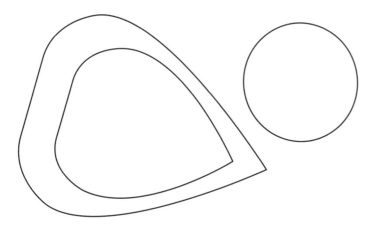

Beg with the large petals, overlap the edges of 2 petals about 1/4 inch (0.5 cm) along the bottom half of the petals. Sew the petals together where they meet with short running sts. Layer the next petal on top of the second petal and sew together. Continue to layer each petal, sewing the first and last petals together to create one round of 6 large petals. Repeat instructions to make a second layer of 6 large petals and a third layer of 5 small petals. Place the small petals on top of both layers of large petals stacked together. For the center, create one stack of buttons as follows: one fabric circle, one large button, and one small button. Center the stack of buttons on top of the flower and the second fabric circle over the center of the bottom of the lid. Working through all layers, sew the flower, fabric, and buttons to the lid of the container through the buttonholes using a doubled length of orange sewing thread.

Variations

You can easily adjust the size of this container to suit your needs. Work more rounds of increases to make it bigger, and work fewer rounds of increases to make it smaller. To adjust the height of the container, simply adjust the number of even rnds.

For a decorative edging, work a blanket stitch (see page 65) around the edge of the lid with a red wool yarn.

This pattern is suitable for all types of fiber as long as the sts are kept small and tight. Try it in 1 mm hemp using a 3.75 mm hook for a small container suitable for a piece of chocolate.

To make a flat lid, use the larger hook and follow the pattern for the base of the container through Rnd 5. Finish by working one round of sl sts in each st. Fasten off and weave in loose ends.

If you don't have a wool sweater or scarf to recycle, crochet your own fabric, then felt it. Using 100% wool in red and cream and a size 5.5 mm (I/9) hook, crochet an 18-inch (45.5 cm) square in hdc using the flo. Work 8 inches (20 cm) of the square alternating two rows of red with two rows of cream. Work the remainder of the square in red. Felt according to the instructions on page 44 and use the felted fabric for the petals and center.

Sew buttons or beads to the lid.

RED'S GOODIE BASKET

Red is absolutely my favorite color. It's bold, confident, and stylish. And so I couldn't resist picking up this spool of bright red leather cording. The inspiration for this pattern came from a beautiful woven basket in my room that I often use to store freshly wound balls of yarn. I figured I could use more than one basket, especially when there are so many fiber goodies in the world to be stashed. I like to imagine that Little Red Riding Hood would use a basket just like this one for her stash. This colorful leather basket is roomy enough for a couple of WIPs (works in progress) and stylish enough to store right in your living room.

Finished Size

10" (w) x 7 1/2" (h) [25.5 cm x 19 cm]

Materials

12 spools round (2 mm) leather cord (100% leather; 25 yards [23 m]; 2.9 ounces [85 g]) in red

Size 6.5 mm (K/10 1/2) hook

Stitch marker

Large-eye yarn needle

Gauge

10 sc x 13 rows = 4" (10 cm)

Design Notes

- The basket begins as a flat circle, then rounds using the principles of concave circles (see page 87). Once the handles are formed, you work multiple increases to flare the upper edge outward.

- This pattern is worked in a spiral without joining the end of each round. Using a stitch marker in the first stitch of each round will help you keep track of the rounds. Each time you come to the stitch marker, begin a new round and move the marker up to the new first stitch.

Stitch Guide

Sc2tog: (Insert hook in next st and draw up a loop) twice, yo and draw yarn through all sts on hook.

Sl st-flo: Slip stitch through the front loop only.

Instructions

Make an adjustable ring (see page 38).

Rnd 1: Work 6 sc into center ring, pull loop tight to close.

Rnd 2: Work 2 sc in each st around – 12 sc.

Rnd 3: *Sc in next st, 2 sc in next st; rep from * around – 18 sc.

Rnd 4: *2 sc in next st, sc in each of next 2 sts; rep from * around – 24 sc.

Rnd 5: *Sc in each of next 3 sts, 2 sc in next st; rep from * around – 30 sc.

Rnds 6–13: Continue to work in established patt, working 1 additional st between inc in each rnd. At the end of Rnd 13 you should have 78 sc.

Rnd 14: Sc in each st around.

Rnd 15: *2 sc in next st, sc in each of next 12 sts; rep from * around – 84 sc.

Rnd 16: Sc in each st around.

Rnd 17: *Sc in each of next 13 sts, 2 sc in next st; rep from * around – 90 sc.

Rnds 18–25: Sc in each st around.

Rnd 26: *Sc2tog over next 2 sts, sc in each of next 8 sts; rep from * around – 81 sc.

Rnd 27: Sc in each st around.

Rnd 28: *Sc in each of next 7 sts, sc2tog over next 2 sts; rep from * around – 72 sc.

Rnd 29: Sc in each st around.

Rnd 30: *Sc2tog over next 2 sts, sc in each of next 7 sts; rep from * around – 64 sc.

Rnd 31: Sc in each st around. Do not fasten off.

HANDLES

This is where you do a bit of tricky shaping to customize the basket. First, you add sts evenly around to create a flare at the top, next you shape the handles by changing the st height before and after them, and finally you skip sts to create the handle space.

Rnd 32: *2 sc in next st, sc in each of next 3 sts *, rep from * to * once, **hdc in next st, dc in next st, ch 16, sk next 12 sts, dc in next st, hdc in next st**, rep from * to * 4 times, rep from ** to ** once, rep from * to * twice – 80 sts, incl ch sts.

Rnd 33: Working in each sc and ch st around, *2 sc in next st, sc in each of next 7 sts; rep from * around – 90 sc.

Rnd 34: Sl st-flo in each st around.

Finishing

Fasten off and weave in loose ends with a large-eye needle.

Variations

Adjust the size of the basket by working more or fewer increase rounds at the bottom.

Thick sturdy fibers like sisal and jute could easily replace the leather. Beware the prickly nature of sisal, though. Throw a pretty ball of yarn in a sisal basket and it may get stuck.

Leather cording comes in a few additional colors. Try working one or more stripes of colors throughout the pattern.

LeaTHer Grannies

If you told my grandmother she couldn't wear leather, she'd let you have an earful. Traditional granny squares are one of the most recognized shapes and are typically worked into scarves, bags, and blankets. I traded chunky wool for stylish leather cording to show how you can bend tradition just a little bit to create something truly uncommon. These little leather containers make an unexpected statement when placed on a bathroom counter filled with flowers, plants, or cotton balls or as a tea light holder (in a glass) that illuminates the granny pattern from within. (To make the blue vase shown on the facing page, see Petite Fleur Vases (page 145).

Finished Size

Small: 3" square (7.5 cm)

Large: 5" square (13 cm)

Materials

Small: 1 spool round (2 mm) leather cord (100% leather; 25 yds [23 m]; 2.9 ounces [85 g]) in black

Large: 2 spools round (2 mm) leather cord (100% leather; 25 yds [23 m]; 2.9 ounces [85 g]) in red

Size 6.5 mm (K/10½) hook

Yarn needle (optional)

Gauge

Make the small square to check your gauge; it should be 3" square (7.5 cm).

Design Notes

- In a traditional granny square, the center stitch of the corner group of stitches is replaced with a chain space to create a lacy square. When you work the subsequent rounds, you work the corner stitches into the space instead of a stitch.

- The small size uses only one spool of leather cord, so it's the perfect project for practicing crochet with leather cord.

- Before beginning, wind the leather cord into a ball for more flexibility.

- Weaving the ends in after each square is completed will make the final finishing easier. If there is a tail end that simply won't stay put, add a dab of fabric, leather, or Krazy glue to the end and press the end down inside a stitch to keep it from poking out. Color the cut ends of the leather with a matching permanent marker to help the ends blend in.

Instructions

GRANNY SQUARE (Make 5)

For small and large motif

Ch 7, join with sl st in first ch to form ring.

Rnd 1: Ch 3 (counts as dc), 2 dc into ring, [ch 3, 3 dc into ring] 3 times, ch 1, dc into 3rd ch of beg ch-3.

For small motif

Fasten off and weave in ends.

For large motif

Rnd 2: Ch 3 (counts as dc), 2 dc in space created by dc join, *ch 1, sk next 3-dc group, (3 dc, ch 3, 3 dc) in next ch-3 sp; rep from * twice, ch 1, sk next 3-dc group, 3 dc in same ch-3 sp as beg, ch 3, sl st in 3rd ch of beg ch-3 to join.

Fasten off and weave in loose ends.

Finishing

Beginning with 2 squares, WS together, join one side of each square with a whipstitch (see page 48). Continue to add squares until there are 4 squares in a row. Whipstitch the last square to the first square to create a squared-off tube. Whipstitch the fifth square to one end of the tube to create the base of the box. Weave in any loose ends with a yarn needle, hook, or your fingers.

Variations

Follow the same pattern above, replacing the leather cord with sisal or jute.

For an experiment, crochet the panels with cotton yarn or string, then dip them in fabric stiffener. Once the squares are dry, whipstitch them together as described above.

YO-YO Basket Bag

I have a fantastic open-air market nearby where local farmers sell their crops and crafters sell their handmade creations. I love to shop for my family's produce on the weekend, eating crêpes and sausages and listening to live music as I stroll. This bag's strong and thick sisal twine makes it farmers' market ready and the crocheted fabric strips and fabric flower yo-yos give it more style than a plain ol' canvas bag.

Finished Size

BAG

13" (w) x 10" (h) x 5½" (d) [33 cm x 25.5 cm x 14 cm], excluding handles

YO-YO

3½" (9 cm) in diameter

Materials

1 yard (1 m) cotton fabric in black

3 spools 1-ply, medium-weight sisal bundling twine (100% sisal; 100 yards [91.5 m]) in natural

Size 9.0 mm (N/13) hook

Stitch markers

Sewing needle

Thread in black and red

Safety pin

2 yards (1.8 m) ½-inch-wide (1 cm) cotton filler cord

Tape

1 (8-inch [20 cm]) round plate

1 (8-inch-square [20 cm]) piece scrap fabric in orange and red print

Chalk

1 (1-inch [2.5 cm]) four-holed round button in black

Gauge

9 sc x 10 rows = 4" (10 cm)

Design Notes

- The pattern begins with oval shaping at the base to give the bag roomy depth. Next, you'll work evenly around to make the body of the bag.

- The bag is worked in joined rounds, turning at the end of each round to create a virtually invisible seam.

- The handles are made using thick cotton filler cord inserted into a simple tube of cotton fabric. They are secured in the final round, working the stitches over the handles as you go.

- The sisal is very textured and may get tangled up in your fuzzier clothes. Trim the wayward fibers with scissors to control it.

- A fabric yo-yo starts with a circle of fabric that is roughly twice the size of the finished yo-yo.

- Use a compass or any round object to make a circle on a piece of fabric. I used a salad plate.

- If you plan on making lots of yo-yos, go ahead and make a template on a piece of cardboard or heavy cardstock. Add an additional ¼-inch (0.5 cm) seam allowance to the template so you can just trace and cut.

- The length of the stitch determines how open the center of the yo-yo will be. A ¼-inch-long (0.5 cm) stitch results in an open center and a 1-inch-long (2.5 cm) stitch will close the center up.

Instructions

Cut the black cotton fabric into two ¹/₂-yard (0.5 m) pieces, reserving one ¹/₂-yard piece for the handle and the yo-yos. Cut the other ¹/₂-yard piece into ³/₄-inch (2 cm) strips and join the strips using one of the two methods below.

Method 1: Overlap the short ends of two strips by ¹/₄ to ¹/₂ inch (0.5 to 1 cm) and then hand- or machine-sew the strips together. Repeat with all strips to form one long continuous strand of fabric.

Method 2: Cut two ¹/₂-inch-long (1 cm) slits at both ends of each strip (centered lengthwise about ¹/₄ inch [0.5 cm] from the end). Take one strip (A) and thread it through one slit of a second strip (B). Now thread one end of (A) through the slit at the opposite end of the same strip (A) and pull to tighten, joining A and B together. Continue joining all the strips to form one long continuous strand of fabric.

> **TIP:** To keep your fabric strips from becoming tangled, wind them into a ball after joining and only use about twenty strips at a time.

With sisal twine and the hook, ch 16.

Rnd 1 (RS): Sc in 2nd ch from hook, sc in each of next 13 ch, 3 sc in last ch, turn to work across bottom loops of foundation ch, sc in each of next 13 ch, 2 sc in last ch (the same ch as the first sc), sl st in first sc to join, turn – 32 sc.

Rnd 2: Ch 1, sk sl st, 2 sc in each of next 2 sts, sc in each of next 13 sts, 2 sc in each of next 3 sts, sc in each of next 13 sts, 2 sc in last st, sl st in first sc to join, turn – 38 sc.

Rnd 3: Ch 1, sk sl st, sc in next st, 2 sc in next st, sc in each of next 14 sts, [2 sc in next st, sc in next st] 3 times, sc in each of next 13 sts, 2 sc in next st, sc in next st, 2 sc in last st, sl st in first sc to join, turn – 44 sc.

Rnd 4: Ch 1, sk sl st, sc in next st, 2 sc in next st, sc in each of next 2 sts, 2 sc in next st, sc in each of next 15 sts, [2 sc in next st, sc in each of next 2 sts] 3 times, sc in each of next 13 sts, 2 sc in next st, sc in last st, sl st in first sc to join, turn – 50 sc.

Rnd 5: Ch 1, sk sl st, sc in next st, 2 sc in next st, sc in each of next 16 sts, [2 sc in next st, sc in each of next 3 sts] 3 times, sc in each of next 13 sts, 2 sc in next st, sc in each of next 3 sts, 2 sc in next st, sc in each of last 2 sts, sl st in first sc to join, turn – 56 sc.

Rnd 6: Ch 1, sk sl st, sc in each of next 2 sts, 2 sc in next st, sc in each of next 4 sts, 2 sc in next st, sc in each of next 17 sts, [2 sc in next st, sc in each of next 4 sts] 3 times, sc in each of next 13 sts, 2 sc in next st, sc in each of last 2 sts, sl st in first sc to join, turn – 62 sc.

Rnd 7: Ch 1, sk sl st, sc in each of next 2 sts, 2 sc in next st, sc in each of next 18 sts, [2 sc in next st, sc in each of next 5 sts] 3 times, sc in each of next 13 sts, 2 sc in next st, sc in each of next 5 sts, 2 sc in next st, sc in each of last 2 sts, sl st in first sc to join, turn – 68 sc.

TURN FOR BODY OF BAG

Ch 1, working through blo, sk sl st, sc in each st around, sl st in first sc to join, turn.

BEGIN BODY OF BAG

Rnd 1: Place st marker in front legs of the first st to mark as the RS, ch 1, sk sl st, working through both loops sc in each st around, sl st in first sc to join, turn.

Rnds 2–11: Ch 1, sk sl st, sc in each st around, sl st in first sc to join, turn.

Rnd 12: Ch 1, sk sl st, sc in each st around, change to fabric strips (dropping sisal to WS of the bag), sl st in first sc to join, turn.

Rnd 13: Ch 1, sk sl st, sc in each st around, pick up sisal dropped in previous rnd (fasten off fabric strips), sl st in first sc to join, turn.

Rnds 14–19: Rep Rnd 2.

Rnds 20–22: Rep Rnds 12–14.

Fasten off and weave in loose ends.

Finishing

Lay the bag on its side and press flat. Find the centermost 16 sts along the top edge on the front of the bag. Using st markers, mark the first and last st (there should be 14 sts between them). The marked sts tell you where the handle will extend from the bag and where it will reenter the bag. Place st markers on the back of the bag following the same instructions.

HANDLE

Using the remaining 1/2 yard of fabric, cut 2 pieces of fabric 2 3/4 by 33 inches (7 by 84 cm) long, reserving the leftover fabric for the yo-yos. With RS facing, sew the short end of one piece to the short end of the second piece with a 1/4-inch (0.5 cm) seam allowance to make one long piece that measures 2 3/4 by 65 1/2 inches (7 by 166.5 cm). Fold each short end 1/4 inch (0.5 cm) to the WS of the fabric and sew to keep in place. Fold the fabric in half lengthwise with RS together and sew the long edges together using a 1/4-inch (0.5 cm) seam allowance. Attach a safety pin to one end of the tube and thread it all the

way through to turn the tube RS out. Cut a piece of cotton filler cord to 65 inches (165 cm) and tape the ends to prevent fraying. Thread the cord through the fabric tube until it is flush with the opening at one end of the tube (there should then be 1/2 inch [1 cm] of open fabric at the opposite end of the tube). Insert the end with the flush filler cord into the space at the opposite end of the tube until the two pieces of filler cord meet. Sew the ends together with 1/8-inch (3 mm) backstitches, inserting the needle through some of the filler cord to secure.

Beginning at the left st marker for one side, lay the handle along the top of the previous row and join the sisal with a sl st. Ch 1 over the handle. Working over the handle, sc around to the next marker on the opposite side. Fasten off. Skip 24 inches (61 cm) of handle, then join the twine at the next marker and ch 1. Working over the handle, sc around to the last marker. Fasten off and weave in loose ends. Adjust the strap to hide the seamed end and then pull them out both sides so they are even.

YO-YO FLOWER (Make 3 Black and 1 Red)

Using the round plate, the fabric left over from the handles, and the red fabric scrap, trace three circles onto the black fabric and one circle onto the red fabric with chalk, adding a 1/4-inch (0.5 cm) seam allowance to each. Cut out the circles. Thread a double length of thread through the sewing needle and knot the end. With WS of one circle facing you, begin to fold the edges over 1/4 inch (0.5 cm). Bring the needle up between the back and front of the seam allowance to hide the knot. Sew a running stitch around the circle, folding the hem over 1/4 inch (0.5 cm), pulling the thread and gathering the fabric as you go (see photo on page 105). When you've worked around the whole circle, pull the thread to tighten the gathers (not so tight as to snap the thread!) and fasten off with a couple of sts through the gathers. Repeat for the three remaining circles.

Group the three black yo-yos in a loosely layered triangle and secure them to the bag with black thread. Place the red yo-yo in the center of the three black yo-yos and place the button in the center. Using the red thread, sew the center yo-yo to the bag through the button holes.

Variations

The handles can be easily replaced with 1/2-inch (1 cm) draw-string cord, 1/2-inch (1 cm) rope made from felted roving, 1/2-inch (1 cm) plastic tubing, or even store-bought handles.

This pattern is easy to size up or down. Work a few more rounds of increases at the base to make it bigger or a few less to make it smaller. Adjust the number of even rounds at the end to change the height.

Fabric yo-yos are so easy and quick to make, you could find yourself with a dozen or so before you know it. Feel free to cover the bag with a bunch of yo-yo flowers in a variety of colors to make your own flower basket.

STRAPPY CLUTCH

I love how cream-colored cotton allows the various stitches and textures to stand out. I created this strappy little clutch to show off the lines created when you work a piece diagonally. After making the main panel, I played around with ways to highlight the diagonal texture using fabric strips. This cute little bag is the perfect size for a wallet, keys, and lipstick.

Finished Size

Before construction: 8" (w) x 15" (h) [20 cm x 38 cm], excluding strap

After construction: 8" (w) x 5" (h) [20 cm x 13 cm], excluding strap

Materials

300 feet (91.5 m) kitchen string

Size 4.5 mm (G/7) hook

Stitch marker

Yarn needle

1/4 yard (0.2 m) lining fabric in dark orange floral pattern

2 (3 x 14 1/2-inch [7.5 cm x 37 cm]) pieces scrap fabric in brown and light orange floral

Pins

1 (14-inch [35.5 cm]) piece lace trim

1 (14-inch [35.5 cm]) piece floral trim

Sewing needle

Thread in brown, dark orange, and light orange, or colors to match the scrap and lining fabrics

Magnetic snap closure in antique brass

Gauge

14 sts x 13 rows = 4" (10 cm), in alternating rows of sc and hdc

Design Notes

- The pattern is a basic rectangle that starts with increases from the point of a triangle, then decreases from the base of another triangle. One side of the bag is lined and then folded into thirds and sewn along two sides.

- Crocheted stripes and strips of fabric work to highlight the diagonal texture of the stitch pattern.

- If you will be hand sewing, use back-stitches (see page 47) to seam the fabric pieces.

- The magnetic snap I used was recycled from a leather bag I deconstructed for materials. Magnetic snaps are easy to find at your local fabric shop.

- The turning chain of the single crochet row does not count as a stitch.

Stitch Guide

I experimented with decrease methods and ended up using two types of decreases in this pattern. At the beginning of each row, skip the first stitch and begin the row in the second stitch. At the end of the row, work two stitches together.

Hdc2tog (modified): Yo, (insert hook in next st and draw up a loop) twice, yo and draw yarn through all four sts on hook. Note: A typical hdc dec would require a yo before inserting the hook into each st of the dec, which results in 5 loops on the hook before the last step. I found that omitting one yo helps shape the edge of the row.

Sc2tog: (Insert hook in next st and draw up a loop) twice, yo and draw yarn through all loops on hook.

Sc3tog: (Insert hook in next st and draw up a loop) 3 times, yo and draw yarn through all loops on hook.

Instructions

FIRST TRIANGLE

Ch 2.

Row 1 (RS): Work 3 sc in 2nd ch from hook, place a marker in the front legs of the last st to mark the RS of the fabric and the bottom edge of the bag, turn – 3 sc.

Row 2 (WS): Ch 1, 2 sc in first st, sc in next st, 2 sc in last st, turn – 5 sc.

Row 3: Ch 2 (counts as hdc), hdc in first st, hdc in each st across to last st, 2 hdc in last st, turn – 7 hdc.

Row 4: Ch 1, 2 sc in first st, sc in each st across to last st, 2 sc in last st, turn – 9 sc.

Repeat Rows 3 – 4 for patt until bottom edge measures 8 inches (20 cm) across; end with a RS row.

SHAPE THE MIDDLE

Continue to work in pattern, alternating rows of sc with rows of hdc, except shape the right and left edges as follows.

Row 1 (WS): Ch 1, sk the first st (dec made), sc in next st, sc in each st across to last st, 2 sc in last st, turn.

Row 2: Ch 2 (counts as hdc), hdc in first st, hdc in each st across to last 2 sts, hdc2tog over last 2 sts, turn.

Rep Rows 1 and 2 until longest edge measures 15 inches (38 cm) from beg; end with a WS row.

SECOND TRIANGLE

Row 1 (RS): Ch 1, sk first st, hdc in next st, hdc in each st across to last 2 sts, hdc2tog over last 2 sts, turn.

Row 2: Ch 1, sk first st, sc in next st and in each st across to last 2 sts, sc2tog over last 2 sts, turn.

Rep Rows 1 and 2 until there are 3 sts remaining. Sc3tog over all 3 sts.

Fasten off and weave in loose ends with a yarn needle.

Finishing

Follow the instructions on page 46 to spray block the rectangle to 8 by 15 inches (20 by 38 cm). Set the bag in a warm place to dry completely.

LINING

Cut an 8 by 15-inch (20 by 38 cm) piece of fabric for the lining. Fold the edges 1/4 inch (0.5 cm) to the WS and press with an iron.

WRIST STRAP

Cut a 2 1/2 by 14-inch (6.5 by 35.5 cm) piece of lining fabric for the strap. Fold the fabric in half lengthwise with RS together and pin or press with an iron. Sew the long edges together 1/4 inch (0.5 cm) from the edge. Leave the short ends unfinished. Turn the tube RS out. Press the strap flat with the seam centered on one side.

FABRIC STRIPS

If you use a piece of fabric that doesn't fray on the edges, you won't need to hem it. Simply cut the strip to 1 inch (2.5 cm) wide and 14 inches (35.5 cm) long. If you use fabric that does fray at the edges when cut, cut each strip to 2 1/2 by 14 inches (6.5 by 35.5 cm) and prepare the strip as for the Wrist Strap above.

CONSTRUCTION

Lay the crocheted rectangle flat with RS facing up. Measuring diagonally from the last corner worked, pin the fabric strips and trimmings in place at about 1, 3 1/2, 5, and 6 1/2 inches (2.5, 9, 13, and 16.5 cm) using the diagonal angle of the stitch pattern as a guide. Sew the strips into place with 1/4-inch (0.5 cm) backstitches (see page 47), folding and sewing the short ends of the strips underneath to the WS of the bag for about an extra 1 inch (2.5 cm). Trim any excess fabric from the strips.

With the WS of the bag facing up, pin the lining into place 1/4 inch (0.5 cm) in from the edge of the bag. Fold the bag into thirds to place and attach the magnetic closure. Affix the base of the closure from the RS of the bottom third of the clutch centered 1 1/2 inches (4 cm) from the folded edge. Using the base of the clasp as a guide for placement, affix the top of the clasp to the inside lining of the top third (or flap). Fold the wrist strap in half and sandwich the bottom 2 inches (5 cm) of both ends between the lining and the bag on the left side where the top third meets the middle third and pin into place (see photo below).

Lay the bag flat with WS facing up and sew the lining into place. With RS together, fold the bottom third of the bag up and sew the sides together using the yarn needle and string. Fasten off and weave in ends. Turn the bag RS out.

Variations

To substitute the fibers, use 100 yards (91.5 m) of worsted-weight cotton yarn.

To make the bag wider, continue to repeat Rows 3 and 4 until the bottom edge is as wide as desired. Work additional rows of middle shaping to make it bigger lengthwise.

Ditch the fabric strips and work the bag in crocheted stripes using all the colors of the rainbow. Using a cotton yarn, change colors every two rows.

Random Stripe Tote

Using random stripes to create this tote lets you burn through a stash of scrap fibers without worrying about having enough of any one color. Work with one color until you get tired of looking at it, then pick up a new color. Crocheted raffia is lightweight but durable, making it perfect for a tote bag. Leave the bag unlined for trips to the farmers' market or the beach, or line it for added strength if you want to use the bag on a daily basis.

Finished Size

13" (w) x 12" (h) x 2.5" (d) [33 cm x 30.5 cm x 6.5 cm]

Materials

Papermart Wraffia (100 yards [91.5 m] per spool)

    2 spools in olive (MC)
    1 spool in Terra Cotta (CC)
    1 spool in Sage (CC1)
    1 spool in Gold (CC2)

Size 4.5 mm (G/7) hook

Stitch markers

Large-eye yarn needle

Recycled belt or store-bought bag strap

5 yards (4.5 m) 1/8-inch-thick (3 mm) suede leather lacing in tan

Gauge

13 sc x 15 rows = 4" (10 cm)

Design Notes

- Because we're using multiple colors, the bag is worked in joined rounds to make the color transitions smoother. Working in joined rounds creates a seam down one side.

- The bag's strap is a recycled thrift store belt. The giant O-rings on each end turned the belt into an instant strap with no reconstruction necessary.

- To create post stitches (see photo on page 112), insert the hook between two stitches from either the back or the front, swing around the post of the second stitch and out to the same side again, yarn over, draw a loop all the way through and complete the stitch as usual. Post stitches can be worked on the row immediately below the current row, or lower. In this pattern, you'll be working Front Post Triple Crochet around stitches three rounds below.

Stitch Guide

Fptrc (front post triple crochet): Yo twice, insert hook from front to back around the post of the next sc from 3 rnds below, yo, pull up a loop, [yo, draw through 2 loops on hook] 3 times.

Striping Sequence

Row	Color	Row	Color
1–2	MC	17	MC
3	CC1	18	CC1
4	MC	19	CC
5	CC	20–21	CC2
6	MC	22	CC
7–8	CC2	23–25	MC
9	CC1	26	CC1
10	CC	27	CC
11	MC	28	CC1
12–14	CC1	29	CC2
15	CC2	30–32	CC
16	CC	33–End	MC

Instructions

With MC, ch 35. Begin working in Striping Sequence (see above).

Rnd 1: Sc in 2nd ch from hook and in each ch across to last ch, 3 sc in last ch (place a marker in the 1st and 3rd st of the 3-sc group), continue working around the bottom loops of the foundation chain, sc in each ch across to last ch (same one you worked the first sc into), 2 sc in last ch (place a marker in the first st of the 2-sc group), sl st in first sc to join – 70 sc.

Rnd 2: Ch 1, 3 sc in first st (place a marker in the 2nd st of the 3-sc group), sc in each st around working 3 sc in each marked st (place a marker in the 2nd st of each 3-sc group), change to CC1 and sl st in first sc to join – 78 sc.

Rnds 3–5: Ch 1, sc in each st around working 3 sc in each marked st and moving the marker up to the 2nd st in the 3-sc group, sl st in first sc to join – Rnd 5 is the last rnd of inc. You should have 102 sc at the end of this rnd. If you'd like the bag to be wider and deeper, continue to work inc rnds as established.

Rnd 6: Ch 1, sc in each st around, sl st in first sc to join.

Repeat Rnd 6 until bag measures 12 inches (30.5 cm) high.

Belt loop round: This rnd creates loops for the leather lacing or ribbon. Ch 1, *[fptrc around the post of the sc three rnds below, sk 1 st (behind the fptrc just worked), sc in next st] 3 times, sc in each of next 11 sts; rep from * around, sl st in first st to join.

Repeat Rnd 6 for two more rows, then work one round of sl st in the flo.

Fasten off and weave in ends with a large-eye needle.

RING TABS

Find and mark the center 7 sts on each side of the bag.

Working on one side of the bag at a time, join any color raffia in the first st.

Row 1: Ch 1, sc in each of the first 7 sts, turn.

Rows 2–8: Ch 1, sc in each st across, turn.

Fasten off with a 6-inch (15 cm) tail. Fold the tab through one strap ring and 1½ inches (4 cm) to the inside of the bag (see photo at right). Working through all layers, sew the tab to the bag across two rows to secure. Weave in any loose ends. Repeat for second side.

Cut 4 laces to 30 inches (76 cm) each and one lace to 60 inches (152.5 cm). Attach two of the shorter laces to each ring with an overhand knot. Thread the long piece through the belt loops and tie both ends together, at the center front, with an overhand knot.

Variations

Substitute worsted-weight cotton or medium-weight jute for the raffia.

If the bag is made in a solid color it can be worked in a spiral without joining at each end; this has the advantage of being seamless.

To crochet your own strap, you need 100 to 200 yards (91.5 to 183 m) of fiber (depending on the desired length of the strap) and two 2- to 3-inch rings (5 to 7.5 cm) (available at craft or fabric stores). First decide how long you want the strap to be, then add 8 inches (20 cm) to the measurement (the extra inches will be folded over the rings). My recycled belt is 2½ inches (6.5 cm) wide and 36 inches (91.5 cm) long, so I would add 8 inches (20 cm) to the length to get 44 inches (112 cm). Make a foundation ch to your predetermined length. Work in rows in sc until the strap is 2 to 3 inches (5 to 7.5 cm) wide, then fasten off. Fold 2 inches (5 cm) of each short end through the rings and sew to secure.

pacific coast basket

Is it a basket or a bag? You decide based on what you need it for. This unconventional basket combines simple crochet stitches and a strong fiber with sturdy hardware—proving that crocheted projects aren't always soft and delicate. Use this basket to hold loaves of bread, market produce, a handmade gift, or a picnic for two.

Finished Size

11" (w) x 5" (h) x 5" (d) [28 cm x 13 cm x 13 cm]

Materials

2 spools 1-ply sisal bundling twine (100 yards [91.5 m] medium-weight 100% sisal per spool) in natural

Size 6.5 mm (K/10½) hook

Yarn needle

2 sheets 10½ x 13½-inch (27 x 34 cm) plastic canvas (optional)

½ yard (0.5 m) blue plaid cotton fabric, for outer lining

½ yard (0.5 m) linen fabric, for inner lining

Pins

Sewing needle

Thread to match inner lining fabric

Chalk

10 (7/16-inch [1 cm]) grommets, in silver

Scissors or hole punch

Grommet-setting tool

Hammer

50 inches (127 cm) 1-inch (2.5 cm) wide cotton webbing trim in brown

2 (1¼-inch [3 cm]) D-rings in silver

Thread to match webbing

Gauge

10 sc x 10 rows = 4" (10 cm)

Design Notes

- This pattern demonstrates how to make the front, base, and back in one piece using back post stitches to turn the corner. An alternative method would be to make separate pieces for the front, back, and base, then whipstitch (see page 48) them together at the end.

- Inserting the plastic canvas form allows the basket to retain its structure even when being carried.

- If you will be hand sewing the fabric, use ⅛ to ¼-inch (3 to 6 mm) backstitches (see page 47).

Stitch Guide

Bpsc (back post single crochet): Working around the body (or post) of the sc from the previous row, insert the hook from back to front to back again, yo and draw through a loop, yo and draw through both loops on the hook (see photo on page 116).

Instructions

MAIN PANEL: FRONT, BASE, AND BACK

With sisal twine and hook, loosely ch 28.

Row 1 (RS): Sc in 2nd ch from hook and in each ch across, turn – 27 sc.

Row 2: Ch 1, sc in each st across, turn.

Rep Row 2 until front measures 5 inches (13 cm) ending on a WS row.

Turn for base: Ch 1, bpsc in each st across, turn.

Rep Row 2 until base measures 5 inches (13 cm) ending on a WS row.

Turn for back: Ch 1, bpsc in each st across, turn.

Rep Row 2 until back measures 5 inches (13 cm) or the same as for front.

Fasten off and weave in loose ends with a yarn needle.

SIDE (Make 2)

Loosely ch 13.

Row 1: Sc in 2nd ch from hook and in each ch across, turn – 12 sc.

Row 2: Ch 1, sc in each st across, turn.

Rep Row 2 until piece measures 5 inches (13 cm).

Fasten off and weave in loose ends.

Finishing

With RS facing, whipstitch one side panel to the main panel. Repeat for second side. Weave in loose ends.

Follow the instructions on page 46 to spray block the piece and shape to finished dimensions. Stuff the main panel with plastic grocery bags to help the basket keep its shape until it is completely dry.

PLASTIC CANVAS FORM

Cut three 11 by 5-inch (28 by 13 cm) and two 5-inch-square (13 cm) pieces of canvas. The larger pieces make up the front, base, and back of the basket and the two smaller pieces make up the sides. Make sure the pieces will fit snugly in the basket and trim edges as necessary. Lay one long section on top of a second long section and whipstitch along one long edge to join. Open the pieces. With the whipstitched seam facing down, lay the third long section on top of one of the other two and whipstitch the long side to the remaining long side of the second piece. Open up the three pieces and whipstitch around three sides of a 5-inch (13 cm) square to each side of the plastic canvas basket. Insert the plastic form into the crochet basket. With sisal and the yarn needle, sew the top edge of the plastic canvas to the crochet basket with 1/2-inch (1 cm) running stitches (see page 49).

LINING

Cut two 17 by 8-inch (43 by 20 cm) pieces of outer lining fabric and two 17-inch-square (43 cm) pieces of inner lining fabric. With RS together, pin one piece of inner liner to the long edge of one piece of outer liner. Repeat for the remaining piece (if your outer lining fabric has a pattern that has to be right-side up, the outer lining must be below the inner lining fabric when looking at it right-side up). With RS together and beginning with the outer layer, sew the long edges of both pieces together with a 1/2-inch (1 cm) seam allowance, pressing the seam toward the inner lining fabric, to form a tube. Do not turn right side out. With the outer lining at the top, slide the tube over the basket. Align the top edge of the tube with the top edge of the basket and sew with short backstitches 1/2 inch (1 cm) from the top (make sure the pattern on your outer lining is upside down).

Turn the lining RS out, pulling the fabric up and over the basket. Pushing a 1/2-inch (1 cm) seam allowance to the wrong side, pin and sew the open edge of the inner lining tube together. Push the inner lining into the basket.

To make the grommet band, ease the inner lining 1 1/4 inches (3 cm) out over the top of the outer lining to form a band and pin. Sew the band through all layers 1/4 inch (0.5 cm) from the bottom edge of the band to allow room for the grommets.

GROMMETS

Measure 10 holes equally spaced around the grommet band. With chalk, trace around the inside of the grommet and cut or punch each hole, trimming as necessary to fit the shaft of the grommet through the hole. Attach the grommets per the manufacturer's instructions.

STRAP

For the strap, thread 1 1/4 inches (3 cm) of the cotton webbing through both D-rings and sew with matching colored thread to secure. Weave the other end of the webbing in and out of the grommets and then fold it over 1/2 inch (1 cm) and sew. Thread the end of the webbing through the D-rings to secure like a belt.

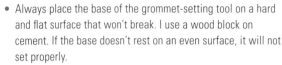

TIPS FOR SETTING GROMMETS
- Always place the base of the grommet-setting tool on a hard and flat surface that won't break. I use a wood block on cement. If the base doesn't rest on an even surface, it will not set properly.
- Hit the grommet-setting tool with a hammer three or four times, then make a quarter turn. Continue to give the setter a few good whacks and rotate until the grommet is set.
- If your fabric is too thin and your grommet does not set properly (meaning, the washer is falling off), use a piece of felt or other thick material to pad the washer. Cut a small piece of felt a little larger than the grommet. Cut a hole out of the center of the felt to fit the shaft of the grommet and place between the washer and the inside of the lining. Set the grommet, then trim off any excess felt.

Variations

Omit the fabric lining and use the crocheted sisal basket to store guest linens in the bathroom, or use with a tea towel to keep your dinner rolls warm on the family table.

If you want to omit the D-ring closure, simply overlap the short ends of the cotton webbing by 1/2 inch (0.5 cm) and sew with matching colored thread.

The size of the basket can be easily adjusted. To adjust the width of the basket, add or remove stitches across. To adjust the depth of the basket, add or remove rows on each side.

geometric pincushions

Because I work on sewing projects all over the house, I need to have pincushions in almost every room. Combining fun with function, these practical little cushions are quick to make and whip up in less than an hour. Further embellish them with grommets, embroidery, ribbons, or brads and give them as gifts to the other crafters in your life. The materials list gives measurements for making one pincushion, but I bet you can't stop at just one. (Pincushions shown from left to right on facing page: triangle, square, oval, and circle.)

Finished Size

Oval: 3" (w) x 2¹/2" (h) x 2" (d) [7.5 cm x 6.5 cm x 5 cm], including the padding

Circle: 2" (w) x 2" (h) [5 cm x 5 cm], including the padding

Square: 2³/4" (w) x 2³/4" (h) [7 cm x 7 cm], including the padding

Triangle: 2¹/2" (w) x 2" (h) [6.5 cm x 5 cm], including the padding

Materials

See individual patterns for fiber and embellishment specifics

Size 4.0 mm (G/7) hook

Large-eye yarn needle

Sewing needle

Plastic canvas (optional)

1 (6 to 8-inch-diameter [15 to 20 cm]) piece scrap fabric, for top

Thread to match the crochet fiber

2 ounces Polyfil stuffing

Gauge

16 sc x 16 rows = 4" (10 cm)

Design Notes

- Make the cushions larger or smaller by adding or removing rounds of increases at the base.

- Sometimes the walls of my pincushion are more flimsy than I want. To keep the walls rigid and structured, switch to a smaller hook size when you begin to work the even rounds or reduce one of the first few even rounds by a few stitches.

- To keep your pins and needles sharp and clean, wrap a piece of steel wool in the stuffing before you construct the cushion.

oval

Materials

25 to 35 feet (7.5 to 10.5 m) thin jute twine in green

Scrap of white yarn (any weight)

Instructions

Ch 6.

Rnd 1: Sc in 2nd ch from hook and in each ch across to last ch, 3 sc in last ch, turn work to continue along the bottom loops of the chain, sc in each ch across to last ch (same ch as the first sc), 2 sc in last ch, sl st in first sc to join – 12 sc.

Rnd 2: Ch 1, 2 sc in first st, sc in each st across to 3-sc group at the end, 2 sc in each st of the 3-sc group, sc in each st across to 2-sc group at the end, 2 sc in each of the 2-sc group, sl st in first sc to join – 18 sc.

Rnd 3: Ch 1, sc in first st, 2 sc in next st, sc in each of next 4 sc, [2 sc in next st, sc in next st] 3 times, sc in each of next 3 sc, 2 sc in next st, sc in next st, 2 sc in last st, sl st in first sc to join – 24 sc.

Rnd 4: Ch 1, sc-blo in each st around, do not join the end of the round.

Rnds 5–8: Continue working sc in one continuous spiral, sl st in next st.

Rnd 9: Sl st in front loop only of each st around.

Fasten off and weave in ends with a large-eye needle.

Weave four strands of the white yarn in and out of each stitch about ¼ inch (0.5 cm) from the top around the container. Fasten off and weave in ends.

See Finishing below to finish the pincushion.

circle

Materials

25 to 35 feet (7.5 to 10.5 m) thin jute twine in burgundy

6¾ inches (17 cm) ½-inch-wide (1 cm) ribbon in pink

Pins

1 skein DMC Six Strand embroidery floss in pink

Embroidery needle

Instructions

Make an adjustable ring (see page 38), ch 1, work 6 sc into ring, and sl st in first sc to join.

Rnd 1: Ch 1, 2 sc in each st around, sl st in first sc to join – 12 sc.

Rnd 2: Ch 1, sc in first st, (2 sc in next st, sc in next st) around, 2 sc in last st, sl st in first sc to join – 18 sc.

Rnd 3: Ch 1, 2 sc in first st, (sc in each of next 2 sts, 2 sc in next st) around, sc in each of last 2 sts, sl st in first sc to join – 24 sc.

Rnd 4: Ch 1, sc-blo in each st around, do not join the end of the round.

Rnds 5–8: Continue working sc in one continuous spiral, sl st in next st.

Rnd 9: Sl st in front loop only of each st around.

Fasten off and weave in ends.

Wrap the ribbon around the cushion, overlapping the ends, and pin in place. Using the embroidery floss and needle, sew the ribbon to the cushion using short running stitches about ⅛ inch (3 mm) from each side.

See Finishing below to finish the pincushion.

square

Materials

5 yards (4.5 m) kitchen string or household twine in white

5 yards (4.5 m) 1-mm round leather cord in brown

1 (½-inch-diameter [1 cm]) four-holed button in brown

White thread

Instructions

Make an adjustable ring (see page 38), ch 1, work 8 sc into ring, and sl st in first sc to join.

Rnd 1: Ch 1, 3 sc in first st, [sc in next st, 3 sc in next st] 3 times, sc in next st, sl st in first sc to join – 16 sc.

Rnds 2–3: Ch 1, sc around working 3 sc in the center stitch of each 3-sc corner group, sl st in first sc to join. Rnd 3 should end with 32 sc.

Rnd 4: Ch 1, sc-blo in each st around, do not join the end of the round.

Rnds 5–8: Continue working sc in one continuous spiral, sl st in next st.

Fasten off and weave in ends.

Join the leather cord in any stitch with a slip stitch. Ch 1, sc in each st around, sl st in first sc to join. Fasten off and weave in ends. Sew button to any side.

See Finishing below to finish the pincushion.

TRIANGLE

Materials

25 to 35 feet (7.5 to 10.5 m) thin jute twine in brown

9 (1/8-inch [3 mm]) grommets

Grommet-setting tool (1/8 inch or 5/32 inch [3 or 4 mm])

Hammer

Brown thread

Instructions

Make an adjustable ring (see page 38), ch 1, work 6 sc into ring, and sl st in first sc to join.

Rnd 1: Ch 1, 2 sc in first st, [sc in next st, 3 sc in next st] twice, sc in next st, sc in same st as first sc of round, sl st in first sc to join – 12 sc.

Rnd 2: Ch 1, 2 sc in first st, [sc in each of next 3 sc, 3 sc in next st] twice, sc in each of last 3 sc, sc in same st as first st of round, sl st in first sc to join – 18 sc.

Rnd 3: Ch 1, 2 sc in first st, [sc in each of next 5 sc, 3 sc in next st] twice, sc in each of last 5 sc, sc in same st as first st of round, sl st in first sc to join – 24 sc.

Rnd 4: Ch 1, sc-blo in each st around, do not join the end of the round.

Rnds 5–8: Continue working sc in one continuous spiral, sl st in next st.

Rnd 9: Sl st in front loop only of each st around.

Fasten off and weave in ends.

Attach three grommets (in spaces between stitches) to each side of the pincushion using the grommet-setting tool. (I arranged mine to look like Swiss cheese.)

Finishing (for all pincushions)

To help your pincushion keep its shape, cut a piece of plastic canvas to fit snugly into the base. Measure the diameter at the base of the container. Cut a piece of scrap fabric twice the size of the base and in the same general shape. With RS of fabric facing you, sew a 1/2-inch (1 cm) running stitch about 1/2 inch (1 cm) in from the edge. Pull the thread to gather the fabric together while stuffing the center with the fiberfill until the cushion is full and firm. Add a couple of sts through the folds to secure and fasten off. Insert the cushion into the container and sew cushion to the top edge of the crocheted piece to secure.

Variation

Forget about the fabric, filling, and pins. Just follow the crochet portion of the pattern to make the cutest little containers for beads, buttons, and coins.

{ 6 }

experiment
Playing with Fiber

If you've made it this far, you're ready to play. In the previous chapters you've learned how to use basic stitches, simple techniques, and uncommon materials to create unique and functional projects. The projects in this chapter were inspired by my personal obsessions with structure and form using traditional and alternative materials and techniques.

I see myself as a functional creator. I don't like having a lot of knick-knacks around the house, so when I make something, it has to have a practical application of some sort—at least most of the time. Occasionally, however, I become taken with the concept of form over function.

The Sushi project (page 135) is a perfect example. My family loves to eat sushi, so the project was a natural extension of something we enjoy doing together. With the sushi mastered, I turned to the Sake Set (page 131), spending night after night stitching and frogging until

I was satisfied. Sometimes you just have to forego the planning process and pick up a hook to see what will happen.

The projects in this chapter (and the tips and techniques that follow) were conceptualized, designed, and mastered through random experimentation. I include my advice here so you don't have to learn the hard way like I did. Actually, sometimes making mistakes is the best way to learn *and* design. Either way, just have fun with this stuff.

PLAYING WITH WIRE

My most recent obsessive period started after a friend inspired me to try crocheting with wire. For one whole week, I wrangled spool after spool of wire, working up several variations on a gold wire circle with beads that would eventually become the Wire Flower (page 143).

Working with wire isn't exactly like working with yarn or other natural fibers. In crochet, we hold pliable fibers by weaving them over and under our fingers to maintain tension. Because tension is already built into wire, you don't need to hold it the same way you hold yarn. The more you bend the wire, the harder and stiffer it becomes until it reaches a breaking point. So the less often you bend the wire, the better.

Try one of these methods for holding the wire to see which is most comfortable for you:

Method 1: For the smallest amount of tension, use only the left thumb and middle finger to pinch and control the wire coming off the spool.

Method 2: For more tension, drape the wire over your left index finger and then pinch it between your thumb and middle finger.

You don't need a slip knot to start the chain when you're working with wire; simply twist it into a loop large enough to fit on the hook. And instead of circling the hook around the wire, use the hand that is holding the wire to wrap it around the hook, and then draw the hook through the chain or stitch. If you try to maintain a tight tension, you will find yourself struggling against the wire. Keep a loose tension and make smooth, deliberate movements. Don't worry about imperfect loops and stitches as you go. The finesse is in the finishing. Once the project is done, block it by using your fingers or pliers to stretch and shape the loops.

Because wire is stiff, it doesn't show texture and pattern very well. Keep to basic, simple stitches like single and double crochet. When planning big wire projects, work it up in stash thread or cheap wire first to avoid the possibility of making a mistake. Unfortunately, mistakes in wire aren't as forgiving as they are when you're using pliable fibers. If you do make a mistake, you can rip back a few stitches by taking them out slowly and carefully. If you have to rip back more than a few stitches, it's best to start over.

Wire will eat your hooks for breakfast, lunch, and dinner, cutting annoying grooves into wood and plastic hooks, and scratching the paint off color-coated metal hooks. Use only steel or uncoated aluminum hooks.

Wire ends can be woven in through the stitches like yarn, but they can also be wrapped around a few wires of a stitch to secure. Be sure to hide and trim any ends to keep them from poking out.

Wire Tools

Simple wire crochet can be done with basic crochet supplies and a sharp pair of scissors. However, the addition of a few wire work supplies can make things easier and more comfortable. These basic tools are available at craft stores.

Wire is used in the Jute Vase (page 127), the Wire Flower (page 143) and the Petite Fleur Vases (page 145).

EMBELLISHING WITH BEADS

Crocheting with beads adds color and texture to any piece. Beads can be sewn on after a project has been crocheted, but they can also be worked into the project as you go. Here are some tips for working with beads:

- Select beads that can be strung onto the fiber you are working with. If your chosen beads don't fit, string them onto a coordinating thread and work the thread together with the fiber, pulling the bead up the thread before completing the stitch.

- Beads must be strung before you begin. This means you have to know how many beads are needed in advance. If you are extremely precise, string exactly what you need. If you like to have some wiggle room, string more than you think you'll need.

- Don't despair if you've run out of beads before you're done. Cut the fiber, add more beads, and weave the ends in.

Beads will always be added to the back of the fabric. This is important to remember because if you are working in the round, then the back side of the fabric will become the right side. If you are working in rows and the project is double sided, you can work beads on both sides. To keep beads on the right side of the fabric only you will have to turn at the end of each row or round and only add them when working on the wrong side.

Beads are used in Sushi (page 135) and the Wire Flower (page 143).

FELTING

The trick to designing a felted project is to figure out how big your pre-felted piece needs to be in order to end up with the desired post-felting size. Start with a test swatch that's at least 5 inches (13 cm) square to get a good shrink assessment. (My default test swatch for worsted-weight wool is a half double crochet stitch pattern created with a 5.5 mm hook and a single strand of yarn.) If you want to experiment with different stitches, hook sizes, and fibers, create separate swatches for each one to see what effect the changes have on the felted result. Be sure to log your results in a stitch diary for future reference. Note the brand of yarn, yarn weight, hook size, and stitch pattern along with the pre-felt and post-felt gauges as described below.

Say you want to make a bag that measures 10 by 12 inches (25.5 by 30.5 cm) after felting.

1. Create a 5-inch-square (13 cm) test swatch using the hook and stitch pattern you will use in the project.

2. Mark off a 4-inch (10 cm) square on the swatch using knotted scraps of a contrasting colored fiber that won't felt (cotton works great).

3. Count and record the number of stitches and rows within the 4-inch (10 cm) square to get the gauge, then divide by 4 to get your gauge per inch. (In this example: $3^1/2$ stitches and 3 rows = 1 inch [2.5 cm].)

4. Felt the test swatch to your desired texture (see photo on page 43).

5. Measure your marked-off square to figure out how much it has shrunk. (In this example: The 4-inch [10 cm] square is now 3 by $3^1/2$ inches [7.5 by 9 cm] after felting.)

6. Divide the final number of inches in width and height by 4 to get the shrink percentage: $3 \div 4 = .75$ (width) and $3^1/2 \div 4 = .875$ (length).

7. Work backward from the shrink percentage to figure out how big the project needs to be before felting. For a bag that will be 10 by 12 inches (25.5 by 30.5 cm): $10 \div .75 = 13.3$ inches (34 cm) wide before felting and $12 \div .875 = 13.7$ inches (35 cm) long before felting.

8. Using the gauge of $3^1/2$ stitches and 3 rows per inch, we can calculate how many stitches and rows we need to work with to make the bag: 13.3 inches (34 cm) x 3.5 stitches per inch = 46.6 (or 47) stitches wide and 13.7 inches (35 cm) x 3 rows per inch = 41.1 (or 41) rows long.

To create this bag, you can either: (1) work two 13.3 by 13.7-inch (34 by 35 cm) panels and sew them together before felting, (2) double the number of stitches in the width and work the bag in a tube to create the front and back at the same time, or (3) double the number of rows to create a long rectangle, fold it in half, and seam the sides.

Felting is used in The Tube Bag (page 57), the Vintage Satchel (page 73), and the Martini Bag (page 153).

THE JOY OF MESH

Crocheted mesh is a lacelike fabric that can be used on its own or combined with other materials for texture, contrast, and structure. A versatile little stitch pattern, mesh creates material for garments, bags, accessories, and home décor. By itself, mesh fabric is lacy and fluid, perfect for an expandable market bag. To make the mesh more structured, use a heavy fiber like jute. Add texture and color by weaving ribbon or strips of fabric through the spaces. To add more interest to the stitch pattern, try filling in a few mesh blocks using the same stitch you are using for the mesh grid.

Mesh is created by alternating stitches with spaces. The height of the spaces is determined by the height of the stitches. You can use singles, doubles, trebles, or any stitch you desire. The width and shape of the spaces are determined by how many chains are made and how many stitches are skipped. When creating the foundation row for the pattern, make sure each mesh pattern repeat will fit.

For example, if you are making a rectangular shape you might work (double crochet in next stitch, chain 3, skip 3 stitches). In order to fit this pattern repeat, the previous row needs to have a multiple of 4 stitches to work from (3 skipped stitches + 1 dc = 4 stitches). If you are working in rows, include one extra stitch in the foundation row to work the last stitch into. If you're working in rounds, you don't need the extra stitch, just join the last chain space to the first stitch.

Mesh is used in the Jute Filet Bag (page 69) and Lace Vases (page 149).

✳   ✳   ✳   ✳   ✳

These projects were designed to be springboards to creativity and I hope they inspire you to try something different the next time you pick up your hook.

jute vase

This project was part of what I like to call my crocheted vase phase, during which I experimented ad nauseam with methods of creating three-dimensional structures from fiber. Despite having its roots in the fibrous plant world, this little vase will stand tall next to its ceramic cousins on the windowsill.

Finished Size

6" (w) x 7" (h) [15 cm x 18 cm]

Materials

125 yards (114 m) Papermart jute twine (2 mm, 1/16 inch wide) in #17 moss green (MC)

72 yards (66 m) 28-gauge wire in gold (CC)

Size 3.75 mm (F/5) hook

Yarn needle

Round balloon, for shaping

Gauge

4 mesh spaces x 3 rounds = 2" (5 cm)

Design Notes

- The wire will help the twine retain its three-dimensional shape.

- The turning chain does not count as a stitch unless instructed otherwise.

Stitch Guide

Dc2tog: [Yo, insert hook in next ch-1 sp, yo, draw up a loop, yo, draw loop through first 2 loops on hook] twice, yo, draw through all loops on hook.

Instructions

Holding one strand of MC and one strand of CC together, make an adjustable ring (see page 38).

Rnd 1: Ch 4 (counts as dc, ch 1), (dc, ch 1) 6 times into ring, dc into ring, hdc in 3rd ch of beg ch-4 to join – 8 ch-1 sps.

Rnd 2: Ch 4 (counts as dc, ch 1), (dc, ch 1) in space made by hdc join, (dc, ch 1) twice in each ch-1 sp around to last ch-1 sp, (dc, ch 1, dc) in last ch-1 sp, hdc in 3rd ch of beg ch-4 to join – 16 ch-1 sps.

Rnd 3: Ch 4 (counts as dc, ch 1), *(dc, ch 1) twice in next ch-1 sp, (dc, ch 1) in next ch-1 sp; rep from * around to last ch-1 sp, (dc, ch 1, dc) in last ch-1 sp, hdc in 3rd ch of beg ch-4 to join – 24 ch-1 sps.

Rnd 4: Ch 4 (counts as dc, ch 1), (dc, ch 1) in sp made by hdc join, *(dc, ch 1) in each of next 2 ch-1 sps, (dc, ch 1) twice in next ch-1 sp; rep from * around to last 2 ch-1 sps, (dc, ch 1) in next ch-1 sp, dc in last ch-1 sp, hdc in 3rd ch of beg ch-4 to join – 32 ch-1 sps.

Rnd 5: Ch 4 (counts as dc, ch 1), *(dc, ch 1) twice in next ch-1 sp, (dc, ch 1) in each of next 7 ch-1 sps; rep from * twice, (dc, ch 1) twice in next ch-1 sp, (dc, ch 1) in each of next 5 ch-1 sps, dc in last ch-1 sp, hdc in 3rd ch of beg ch-4 to join – 36 ch-1 sps.

Rnd 6: Ch 4 (counts as dc, ch 1), (dc, ch 1) in each ch-1 sp around, hdc in 3rd ch of beg ch-4 to join.

Rnds 7–8: Rep Rnd 6.

Rnd 9: Ch 4 (counts as dc, ch 1), (dc, ch 1) in each of next 2 ch-1 sps, *dc2tog over next 2 ch-1 sps, (dc, ch 1) in each of next 4

sts; rep from * around, ending dc2tog over next 2 ch-1 sps, dc in last ch-1 sp, hdc in 3rd ch of beg ch-4 to join – 30 ch-1 sps.

Rnd 10: Ch 4 (counts as dc, ch 1), *dc2tog over next 2 ch-1 sps, (dc, ch 1) in each of next 3 ch-1 sps; rep from * around, ending dc2tog over next 2 ch-1 sps, (dc, ch 1) in next ch-1 sp, dc in last ch-1 sp, hdc in 3rd ch of beg ch-4 to join – 24 ch-1 sps.

Rnd 11: Ch 4 (counts as dc, ch 1), *dc2tog over next 2 ch-1 sps, (dc, ch 1) in each of next 2 ch-1 sps; rep from * around, ending dc2tog over next 2 ch-1 sps, dc in last ch-1 sp, hdc in 3rd ch of beg ch-4 to join – 18 ch-1 sps.

Rnd 12: Ch 2 (counts as hdc), hdc in each ch-1 sp around, sl st in first hdc to join – 18 hdc.

NECK

Rnds 1–4: Ch 1, sc in first st, sc in each st around, sl st in first sc to join.

Rnd 5: Ch 1, 2 sc in first st, *sc in each of next 2 sts, 2 sc in next st; rep from * around, ending sc in each of last 2 sts – 24 sc.

Rnd 6: Ch 1, sc in each st around.

Rnd 7: Ch 1, sc in each of first 2 sts, *2 sc in next st, sc in each of next 2 sts; rep from * around, ending 2 sc in last st – 32 sc.

Rnd 8: Ch 1, 2 sc in first st, *sc in each of next 3 sts, 2 sc in next st; rep from * around, ending sc in each of last 3 sts, sl st in first sc to join – 40 sc.

Fasten off and weave in ends with yarn needle.

Finishing

Holding the open end of the balloon, insert the round end into the vase. Blow up the balloon until the vase is rounded and smooth. Keeping the end of the balloon pinched closed, adjust any stitches that look out of place, then let the air out of the balloon.

sake set

When I tell friends about my crocheted sake sets, they always ask me if the pitcher and glasses really work. Unfortunately, I haven't figured out what kind of material to line these little guys with so you can actually pour sake from them, but maybe someday. Until then, check out real sake sets online or at a store and play with shaping techniques to re-create square, round, or cone-shaped cups and pitchers. Or try a martini or tea set, using the shaping techniques found in chapter 5 as a guide.

Finished Size

Pitcher: 2¹/2" (w) x 5" (h) [6.5 cm x 13 cm]

Cup: 1¹/2" (4 cm) square

Materials

100 yards (91.5 m) cotton string in natural (MC)

1 skein Bernat Handicrafter (100% cotton; 80 yards [73 m]; 1.75 ounces [50 g]; CYCA #4 worsted) in #13628 hot orange (CC)

Size 4.5 mm (G/7) hook

Size 3.75 mm (F/5) hook

Small yarn needle

Gauge

18 sc x 18 rows = 4" (10 cm) using larger hook

Design Notes

- Do not chain one at the beginning of each round.

- As you work, the side facing you is the outside of the pitcher or cup.

- To make the cups curve in a little around the sides, I switched to a smaller hook after completing the base.

Stitch Guide

Sc2tog: (Insert hook in next st and draw up a loop) twice, yo and draw yarn through all loops on hook.

Instructions

PITCHER

Using MC and larger hook, make an adjustable ring (see page 38).

Rnd 1: Work 8 sc into ring, join with a sl st in first sc – 8 sc.

Rnd 2: Sc in first st, *3 sc in next st, sc in next st; rep from * twice, 3 sc in last st, join with sl st in first sc – 16 sc.

Rnd 3: Sc in each of first 2 sts, *3 sc in next st, sc in each of next 3 sts; rep from * twice, 3 sc in next st, sc in last st, join with sl st in first sc – 24 sc.

Rnd 4: Sc in each of first 3 sts, *3 sc in next st, sc in each of next 5 sts; rep from * twice, 3 sc in next st, sc in each of last 2 sts, join with sl st in first sc – 32 sc.

Rnd 5: Working through blo, sc in each st around, join with sl st in first sc.

Rnd 6: Working through both loops, sc in each st around, join with sl st in first sc.

Rnd 7: Sc in each st around, change to CC, join with sl st in first sc.

Rnds 8–14: Sc in each st around, join with sl st in first sc.

Rnd 15: Sc in each of first 2 sts, *sc2tog over next 2 sts, sc in each of next 6 sts; rep from * twice, sc2tog over next 2 sts, sc in each of the last 4 sts, join with sl st in first sc – 28 sc.

Rnd 16: Rep Rnd 6.

Rnd 17: Sc in each of first 3 sts, *sc2tog over next 2 sts, sc in each of next 5 sts; rep from * twice, sc2tog over next 2 sts, sc in each of the last 2 sts, join with sl st in first sc – 24 sc.

Rnd 18: Rep Rnd 6.

Rnd 19: Sc in each of first 2 sts, *sc2tog over next 2 sts, sc in each of next 4 sts; rep from * twice, sc2tog over next 2 sts, sc in each of the last 2 sts, change to MC, join with sl st in first sc – 20 sc.

Rnd 20: Rep Rnd 6.

Rnd 21: Sc in each of first 3 sts, *sc2tog over next 2 sts, sc in each of next 3 sts; rep from * twice, sc2tog over next 2 sts, sc in last st, join with sl st in first sc – 16 sc.

Rnd 22: Rep Rnd 6.

Rnd 23: Sc in each of first 2 sts, *sc2tog over next 2 sts, sc in each of next 2 sts; rep from * twice, sc2tog over next 2 sts, join with sl st in first sc – 12 sc.

Rnd 24–25: Rep Rnd 6.

Rnd 26: Sc in each of first 2 sts, *2 sc in next st, sc in each of next 2 sts; rep from * twice, 2 sc in next st, join with sl st in first sc, turn – 16 sc.

Rnd 27: Ch 1, sc in joining sl st, sc in each of next 2 sts, 2 sc in next st, sc in each of next 3 sts, 3 sc in next st (forms the pouring spout), *sc in each of next 3 sts, 2 sc in next st; rep from * once, join with sl st in first sc – 21 sc.

Fasten off and weave in loose ends with yarn needle.

CUPS (Make 4)

Using larger hook and MC, make an adjustable ring.

Rnd 1: Work 8 sc into ring, join with a sl st in first sc – 8 sc.

Rnd 2: Sc in first st, *3 sc in next st, sc in next st; rep from * twice, 3 sc in last st, join with sl st in first sc – 16 sc.

Rnd 3: Sc in each of first 2 sts, *3 sc in next st, sc in each of next 3 sts; rep from * twice, 3 sc in next st, sc in last st, join with sl st in first sc – 24 sc.

Rnd 4: Working through the blo, sc in each st around, join with sl st in first sc.

Rnd 5: Working through both loops, sc in each st around, change to CC, join with sl st in first sc.

Rnd 6–7: Sc in each st around, join with sl st in first sc.

Rnd 8: *Switch to smaller hook,* sc2tog over first 2 sts, *sc in each of next 4 sts, sc2tog over next 2 sts; rep from * twice, sc in each of the last 4 sts, change to MC, join with sl st in first sc – 20 sc.

Rnd 9: Work 2 sc in first st, *sc in each of next 4 sts, 2 sc in next st; rep from * twice, sc in each of last 4 sts, join with sl st in first sc – 24 sc.

Fasten off and weave in loose ends with yarn needle.

Variation

The pattern can be made using one or more colors. I think my next one will be stripes of multiple colors.

Embroider a Japanese symbol or design on the front of the pitcher. Any embellishments, including embroidery or buttons, need to be added before forming the narrow neck at the top of the pitcher (around Rnds 16–17), otherwise the opening becomes too small to work through. I made the blue and brown version shown here with a round base. Start with 8 sc in an adjustable ring and work a circle in sc as directed on page 87 for four rnds (for the pitcher) and three rnds (for the cups). Follow the pattern above beg with Rnd 5 (for the pitcher) and Rnd 5 (for the cups). I embroidered a little tree using wool yarn and French knots (see page 153) for flowers.

Substitute 50 to 100 yards (46 to 91.5 m) of double-knit (dk) to worsted-weight cotton yarn, lightweight jute twine, hemp, or raffia . . . even acrylics would work as long you play with the hook size to ensure your stitches are tight.

SUSHI

Mmmmm, sushi. These tasty little bites are super fast and easy to make. Each layer consists of a simple rectangle that is rolled or folded to create a yummy sushi treat. Use them as table decorations for a party or add them to gifts as creative package toppers. If you finish them off with a little loop through the center you'll have the most unique holiday ornaments on the block. The materials list gives measurements for making one California roll and one Tamago roll.

Finished Size

California Roll: 1$^{1/2}$" (w) x 1" (h) [4 cm x 2.5 cm]

Tamago Roll: 1$^{1/2}$" (w) x 1" (h) [4 cm x 2.5 cm]

Materials

Lily Sugar 'n Cream (100% cotton; 120 yards [109 m]; 2.5 ounces [70 g]; CYCA #4 worsted)

    10 to 20 yards (9 to 18 m) #1 white
    10 to 20 yards (9 to 18 m) #2 black
    3 to 5 yards (2.7 to 4.5 m) #10 yellow

5 yards (4.5 m) Patons Classic Merino (100% wool; 223 yards [205 m], 3.5 ounces [100 g]; CYCA #4 worsted) in #238 paprika

Knitpicks Wool of the Andes (100% Peruvian Highland Wool; 110 yards [100.6 m]; 1.75 ounces [50 g]; CYCA #4 worsted)

    5 yards (4.5 m) #439 grass
    5 yards (4.5 m) #766 avocado

Size 3.75 mm (F/5) hook

Small yarn needle

Gauge

18 sc x 18 rows = 4" (10 cm)

Design Notes

- Each piece is a rectangle that is folded or rolled and sewn together.

- The turning chain does not count as a stitch.

CALIFORNIA ROLL

Instructions

IMITATION CRAB FILLING

With white yarn, ch 5.

Row 1: Sc in 2nd ch from hook and in each ch across, turn – 4 sc.

Row 2: Ch 1, sc in each st across, turn.

Rep Row 2 working a total of 7 rows in white, then 3 rows in paprika, for a piece that measures about 2$^{1/2}$ inches (6.5 cm) long. Fasten off and weave in ends with yarn needle.

AVOCADO AND CUCUMBER FILLING

With avocado yarn, ch 5.

Row 1: Sc in 2nd ch from hook and in each ch across, turn – 4 sc.

Row 2: Ch 1, sc in each st across, turn.

Rep Row 2 working a total of 4 rows in avocado, then 4 rows in grass, for a piece that measures about 2 inches (5 cm) long. Fasten off and weave in ends.

RICE

With white yarn, ch 5.

Row 1: Sc in 2nd ch from hook and in each ch across, turn – 4 sc.

Row 2: Ch 1, sc in each st across, turn.

Rep Row 2 for 11 rows or until piece measures about 3 inches (7.5 cm). Fasten off, leaving a 6-inch (15 cm) tail for sewing.

NORI

With black yarn, work as for Rice for 15 rows or until piece measures 4 inches (10 cm).

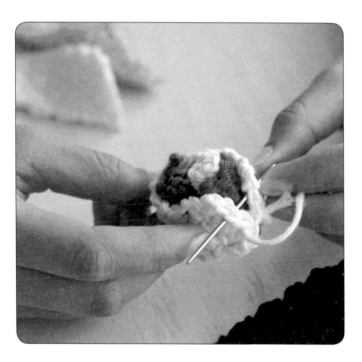

Finishing

Roll crab piece up beg with the short white end and ending with the crab. Roll each short end of the avocado/cucumber piece in toward the center.

Holding filling pieces together, wrap the rice around the filling and sew short ends together, catching a bit of filling in the sts to secure (see photo below).

Wrap nori around rice roll and sew ends together, catching a bit of the rice in the sts to secure. Weave in loose ends.

TAMAGO ROLL

Instructions

RICE

With white yarn, ch 7.

Row 1: Sc in 2nd ch from hook and in each ch across, turn – 6 sc.

Row 2: Ch 1, sc in each st across, turn.

Rep Row 2 until piece measures 4 inches (10 cm). Fasten off, leaving a 6-inch (15 cm) tail for sewing.

Roll short end over 3 times widthwise and whipstitch (see page 48) last row to folded edge. Fasten off and weave in ends.

CROCHETED EGG

With yellow yarn, ch 12.

Row 1: Sc in 2nd ch from hook and in each ch across, turn – 11 sc.

Row 2: Ch 1, sc in each st across, turn.

Rep Row 2 until piece measures 2 inches (5 cm).

Fold in half widthwise and and sl st long edges together. Fasten off and weave in ends.

Lay egg on top of rice.

NORI

With black yarn, ch 14 or until piece wraps around center of egg and rice.

Row 1: Sc in 2nd ch from hook and in each ch across, turn – 13 sc.

Rows 2–3: Ch 1, sc in each st across, turn.

Finishing

Wrap nori around the egg and rice. Sew ends of nori together, catching a bit of the rice in the sts to secure. Fasten off and weave in ends.

Variations

An inside-out California roll is just a standard California roll with the nori wrapped around the filling and the rice on the outside. Sometimes, the roll is served topped with toasted sesame seeds or fish eggs. To make an inside-out California roll, simply use black yarn for the rice instructions above and white yarn for the nori instructions above. Thread 50 to 100 orange seed beads on orange thread for fish eggs (or use beige seed beads and beige thread for sesame seeds) and sew them onto the outside of the roll.

Use the patterns here to make your own tasty sushi creations, like spider rolls or sashimi.

corde market bag

The lace motifs in this bag remind me of barnacles, spider-webs, and Swiss cheese. An adaptation of the traditional string market bag, this pattern uses an open foundation ring to create lacy motifs that you join together as you go. The motifs are added in staggered rows from side to side. The final row joins to the first row to create a tube. Add a few half motifs to even out the bottom edge, then seam it together to make the bottom of the bag.

Finished Size

12" (w) x 18" (h) [30.5 cm x 46 cm]

Materials

300 yards (274.5 m) 100% cotton medium-weight kitchen string or twine

Size 4.25 mm (G/6) hook

Yarn needle

2 1/2 yards (2.3 m) 1/8-inch-thick (3 mm) leather lacing in dark brown

Gauge

One motif = 5" (13 cm) in diameter

Design Notes

- This pattern does require some concentration. Keep the motifs laid out on a flat surface, RS up, as you join them to make sure they are being joined to the next motif in the correct arches.

Instructions

LAYOUT

Working horizontally, build 6 staggered rows with 3 motifs in each row. The first 5 rows should each consist of 1 dense motif and 2 lacy motifs; the sixth row consists of lacy motifs only. Join the first row of motifs to the sixth to create a tube. To create an even edge at the bottom, fill in the empty spots of every other row with a half motif.

JOINING THE MOTIFS

Join the motifs as you create them. Each motif is joined in the third rnd by two arches on each side. It sounds more difficult than it is, and once you get the hang of it, the project will go quickly.

Create the first motif (Motif A) without joining to anything. Once you reach the third rnd of the second motif (Motif B): Work the first 3 chains for one ch-7 arch of Motif B, sl st in the 4th, or center ch, of a corresponding arch on Motif A, pulling the yarn through the ch on Motif A and the loop on the hook. Ch 3, sc in 3rd ch of next ch-5 arch of Motif B. Repeat this process to connect the next arch of both Motif B and the corresponding arch on Motif A. Complete the joining rnd for Motif B and begin the third motif, joining the third motif to Motif B in the two arches opposite Motif A. With the first few motifs you will only be joining 2 motifs together. As you build the bag, the motif you are working on will need to join to 2 or more motifs, with the final motif joining on all sides.

As you get further along the bag, you might find that you've skipped over an arch or you need to undo a joining rnd in order to add another motif. It's easy to unjoin a motif, even if it's in the middle of the bag. Simply find the ending tail and unknot. Carefully pull the tail end to unravel the chains and stitches until you're past the problem area, then rework the joining round and fasten off.

Fill in the bottom spaces at the end of every other round by joining 2 half motifs B and 1 half motif A to make the bottom edge straight across.

FULL MOTIF A
(Lace)

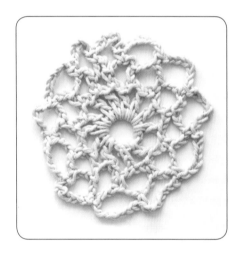

With string and hook, ch 12, sl st in first ch to form ring.

Rnd 1: Ch 6 (counts as dc, ch 3), dc into ring, work (ch 3, dc) into ring 10 times, ch 1, dc in 3rd ch of beg ch-6 (counts as last ch-3 sp) – 12 ch-3 arches.

Rnd 2: Ch 1, sc in same dc, (ch 5, sc in center ch of next ch-3 sp) around, ch 2, tr in first sc (counts as last ch-5 sp) – 12 ch-5 arches.

Joining Rnd 3: Ch 1, sc in same tr, (ch 7, sc in center ch of next ch-5 sp) around, ending ch 7, sl st in first sc to join – 12 ch-7 arches. Fasten off.

FULL MOTIF B
(Dense Center Circle)

Ch 14.

Rnd 1: Ch 3 (counts as dc), work 35 dc into ring, sl st in 3rd ch of beg ch-3 – 36 dc.

Rnd 2: Ch 1, sc in first st, (ch 5, sk next 2 dc, sc in next dc) around until 2 dc rem, ch 2, tr in first sc to join – 12 ch-5 arches.

Joining Rnd 3: Ch 1, sc in tr, (ch 7, sc in 3rd ch of next ch-5) around ending ch 7, sl st in first sc to join – 12 ch-7 arches. Fasten off.

HALF MOTIF A (Lace)

Ch 12, sl st in first ch to form ring.

Rnd 1: Ch 6 (counts as dc, ch 3), dc into ring, (ch 3, dc) into ring 6 times, turn – 7 ch-3 arches.

Rnd 2: Ch 5, (sc in center ch of next ch-3 sp, ch 5) around ending ch 2, tr in 5th ch of beg ch-6, turn – 7 ch-5 arches.

Joining Rnd 3: Ch 1, sc in same st, (ch 7, sc in center ch of next ch-5 sp) around – 6 ch-7 arches. Fasten off.

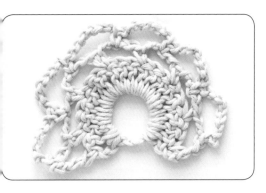

HALF MOTIF B (Dense Center Circle)

Ch 14.

Rnd 1: Ch 3 (counts as dc), work 22 more dc into ring, turn – 23 dc.

Rnd 2: Ch 1, sc in same st, (ch 5, sk next 2 dc, sc in next dc) around ending ch 2, tr in last st (counts as last ch-5 sp), turn – 7 ch-5 arches.

Joining Rnd 3: Ch 1, sc in same st, (ch 7, sc in center ch of next ch-5) around – 6 ch-7 arches. Fasten off.

> **TIP:** You can also just work the joining sl st into the ch-7 space of the next motif if it's too tedious to work directly into the center ch.

Finishing

Turn the bag inside out and lay flat. With bottom edges pressed together and working through both layers, sc evenly across through the unjoined arches and dc posts along the edge to create the seam.

Fasten off and weave in loose ends with yarn needle. Turn RS out.

Join yarn through any free arch along the top edge and ch 1. Sc evenly along the top edge working 7 sc in the spaces of the unjoined arches and 3 sc in the spaces of the joined arches. Fasten off and weave in loose ends.

Weave leather lacing through the arches along the top edge. Leaving about 5 inches (13 cm) free, knot the two ends together with an overhand knot.

Variations

Cotton, linen, or 1-mm jute twine would be great substitutions for the kitchen string in this bag.

Increase the size of your bag by simply adding more motifs. Adding motifs to each row will make your bag longer; adding more rows of motifs will make it wider.

To make the top edge of the bag a straight edge, work an additional 3 half motifs and join them as you did for the bottom edge.

wire flower

This is a good starter project if you're interested in working with wire. The flower is quick and easy to make and can be worn as a pin, on a chain as a pendant, or attached anywhere you need a little touch of gold. The petals are made with a simple, adjustable loop and the number of beads or layers of petals can be changed to increase or decrease the size of the flower to your taste.

Finished Size

3¹/₂" (w) [9 cm]

Materials

7 (6-mm) round semiprecious or glass beads in turquoise

1 spool (30 yards [27.5 m]) 24-gauge Beadsmith Craft tarnish-resistant wire in gold

1 spool (30 yards [27.5 m]) 24-gauge Beadsmith Craft tarnish-resistant wire in copper

Size 4.25 mm (G/7) hook

Small pin backing in gold

Gauge

Checking the gauge isn't essential for this project; if you want to check your progress, the first layer should be 3" (9 cm) in diameter.

Design Notes

• This pattern is made in a spiral; do not join at the end of the round.

Stitch Guide

Bsc: Insert hook into ring, yo, draw up a loop, bring bead up to ring, yo, draw through both loops on hook.

Instructions

FIRST LAYER

String the beads onto the gold wire. Make a loop ¹/₂ inch (1 cm) in diameter and twist the base of the loop 2 times to secure. Insert the hook through the ring and draw up a loop, ch 1.

Rnd 1: Work 7 bsc into ring.

Rnd 2: Working through flo of the previous rnd, [insert hook in next st, yo and draw up a loop to about ³/₄ inch (2 cm) long, remove the hook from the loop, twist the base of the loop 2 or 3 times] 7 times – 7 petals.

Fasten off, leaving a 6-inch tail (15 cm).

SECOND LAYER

With copper wire, make a loop ¹/₂ inch (1 cm) in diameter and twist the base of the loop 2 times to secure. Insert the hook through the ring and draw up a loop, ch 1.

Rnd 1: Work 7 sc into ring.

Rnd 2: Rep Rnd 2 from first layer, pulling each loop to 1¹/₄ inches (3 cm) long.

Fasten off, leaving a 6-inch (15 cm) tail.

Finishing

Lay the first layer of petals on top of the second layer of petals. Using the tail end, whipstitch (see page 48) the tail through the stitches and around the center of both layers to secure. Secure the pin back using the second tail end or an extra length of wire.

After pulling and wrapping, your flower may be in need of a little TLC. Using your fingers, open the petals and smooth out any kinks.

Variations

The loops on each petal are adjustable; pull them out to make longer or shorter petals.

Add more beads or extra layers.

Make 2 of the first layer only with short loops, then attach to a pair of earring hooks by securing a jump ring to the back of the first round.

petite fleur vases

I live in the Pacific Northwest, where it is dark and gloomy for about nine months out of the year. By the time April rolls around, I'm impatient for signs of spring. This petite vase is the perfect vessel for a single little flower to remind me that sunny days are on the way. You can make this vase with just about any material, including leather, string, hemp, or wire.

Finished Size

3³/₄" (h) [9.5 cm]

Materials

35 yards (32 m) 1-mm round leather cord in blue (see photo on page 98), or

35 yards (32 m) medium-weight household string in white, or

35 yards (32 m) 1-mm (20#) hemp twine in pink

Size 3.75 mm (F/5) hook

Yarn needle

Small glass or plastic tube to fit inside the vase (optional; see design notes)

Gauge

18 sc x 22 rows = 4" (10 cm) using leather, string, or hemp

Design Notes

- This pattern is worked in a spiral, so you will not join stitches at the end of the round. All of the stitches should be tight except for the wire. If you are using wire, hold it loosely and allow it to flow freely through the hook.

- To help keep track of your rounds, use a stitch marker or scrap of contrasting colored yarn to mark the first stitch of each round. When you come around to the first stitch, move the marker to the first stitch of the next round.

- If you want to use these vases for real flowers, insert a glass or plastic vial (something that holds water) into the vase. I used ¹/₂-inch (1 cm) plastic tubing and a rubber stopper from my local home improvement store. Plastic tubing can be easily cut to fit your vase. Other ideas: use the lid from a lipstick tube, a Chapstick tube with the Chapstick removed, or travel aspirin containers. If you just can't find the right size container, see Variations below for tips on adjusting the size of the crocheted vase. If your vial is too short, fill the base of the crocheted vase with beans or beads until the container is the correct height.

Stitch Guide

Sc2tog: [insert hook in next st, yo, draw up a loop] twice, yo, pull a loop through all loops on the hook.

Instructions

Make an adjustable ring (see page 38).

Rnd 1: Ch 1, work 6 sc into ring – 6 sc.

Rnd 2: Work 2 sc in each st around – 12 sc.

Rnd 3: *Sc in next st, 2 sc in next st; rep from * around – 18 sc.

Rnd 4: *2 sc in next st, sc in each of next 2 sts; rep from * around – 24 sc.

Rnd 5: *Sc in each of next 3 sts, 2 sc in next st; rep from * around – 30 sc.

Rnds 6–10: Sc in each st around.

Rnd 11: *Sc2tog over next 2 sts, sc in each of next 3 sts; rep from * around – 24 sc.

Rnd 12: Rep Rnd 6.

Rnd 13: *Sc in each of next 2 sts, sc2tog over next 2 sts; rep from * around – 18 sc.

Rnd 14: Rep Rnd 6.

Rnd 15: *Sc2tog over next 2 sts, sc in next st; rep from * around – 12 sc.

Rnds 16–18: Rep Rnd 6.

Rnd 19: *2 sc in next st, sc in each of next 2 sts; rep from * around – 16 sc.

Rnd 20: *Sc in each of next 3 sts, 2 sc in next st; rep from * around – 20 sc

Rnds 21–23: Rep Rnd 6.

Sl st in each of next 2 sts. Fasten off and weave in loose ends with a yarn needle.

Finishing

Make a dent with your thumb in the center ring at the bottom of the vase to help it sit flat. Insert the glass or plastic tube, add a little water and a flower, and you're done.

Variations

To increase or decrease the width of the vase, work additional rounds at the base, increasing each round by 6 stitches (to make it wider) or work fewer rounds of increases (to make it skinnier). Work an increased or decreased number of even rounds (Round 6) to make the vase taller or shorter.

To make a hemp and copper wire vase, you need 15 yards (14 m) of 20-pound Hemp Basics hemp twine in #4000 black, 24 yards (22 m) of Elite Better Beads 28-gauge metallic wire in copper, and 3.75 (F/5) and 4.5 (G/7) hooks. Beginning with the hemp and the smaller hook, work the above pattern through Round 9. Switch to the copper wire and the larger hook for the remainder of the pattern. When crocheting with wire, hold the wire loosely and do not pull the stitches to tighten.

You can use any fiber you want with this pattern, but you might not get the sizes shown. Adjust the size of your hook if you change fibers. You don't want to hurt your hands when working the stitches, but you do need to keep the stitches as tight as you comfortably can to help the vase keep its structure.

lace vases

After being inspired by a stylish arrangement of ceramic vases, I designed these crocheted vases to see whether I could make lace containers that stand up on their own. First I was going to make my own rubber molds and learn to mix up resins, then I took my plans down a few necessary notches and dipped the crocheted vases in fabric stiffener. This project is fast, easy, and, best of all, doesn't require a hazardous materials mask. (Vases shown from left to right on facing page: kitchen string, jute, and hemp.)

Finished Size

Hemp (off-white; open base): 2¹/₂" (w) x 5" (h) [6.5 cm x 13 cm]

Kitchen String (white; closed base): 2" (w) x 5" (h) [5 cm x 13 cm]

Jute (brown; closed base): 3" (w) x 6" (h) [7.5 cm x 15 cm]

Materials

See individual patterns for fiber and hook specifics

Aleene's Fabric Stiffener & Draping Liquid

Plastic mesh canvas or glass, for shaping

Gauge

Hemp: 3 mesh spaces x 2 rnds = 1¹/₂" (4 cm)

Kitchen String: 3¹/₂ mesh spaces x 3 rnds = 2" (5 cm)

Jute: 3 mesh space x 2 rnds = 1¹/₂" (4 cm)

Design Notes

- The gauge varies depending on the fiber you use. It's more important to keep the stitches snug.

HEMP

Materials

50 yards (46 m) 1-mm hemp in natural

Size 3.5 mm (E/4) hook

Instructions

OPEN BASE

Fsc 36, leaving a 4-inch (10 cm) tail.

Rnds 1–6: Ch 1, sc in each st around, sl st in first sc to join.

RECTANGLES AND SQUARES MESH PATTERN

Rnd 1: Ch 4 (counts as dc, ch 1), sk next st, (dc in next st, ch 3, sk next 3 sts, dc in next st, ch 1, sk next st) around ending with ch 3, sl st in 3rd ch of beg ch-4 to join.

Rnd 2: Ch 4 (counts as dc, ch 1), sk next ch-1 sp, (dc in next dc, ch 3, sk next ch-3 sp, dc in next dc, ch 1, sk next ch-1 sp) around ending with ch 3, sl st in 3rd ch of beg ch-4 to join.

Rep Rnd 2 until desired height.

Last rnd: Ch 1, sc in same st as sl st, sc around working 1 sc in each dc, 1 sc in each ch-1 sp and 3 sc in each ch-3 sp, sl st in first sc to join.

Fasten off and weave in any loose ends. Follow Finishing instructions to stiffen fiber.

KITCHEN STRING

Materials

50 yards (46 m) 100% cotton medium-weight kitchen string in white

Size 3.5 mm (E/4) hook

Instructions

CLOSED BASE

Rnd 1: Ch 1, 6 sc into ring, sl st in first sc to join – 6 sc.

Rnd 2: Ch 1, 2 sc in each st around, sl st in first sc to join – 12 sc.

Rnd 3: Ch 1, sc in first st, (2 sc in next st, sc in next st) around, 2 sc in last st, sl st in first sc to join – 18 sc.

Rnd 4: Ch 1, 2 sc in first st, (sc in each of next 2 sts, 2 sc in next st) around, ending sc in last st, sl st in first sc to join – 24 sc.

Rnd 5: Ch 1, sc in each of first 3 sts, (2 sc in next st, sc in each of next 3 sts) around, ending 2 sc in last st, sl st in first sc to join – 30 sc.

Rnd 6: Ch 1, 2 sc in first st, (sc in each of next 4 sts, 2 sc in next st) around, ending sc in each of last 4 sts, sl st in first sc to join – 36 sc.

Rnd 7: Ch 1, sc in blo of each st around, sl st in first sc to join.

Rnds 8–10: Ch 1, sc in each st around, sl st in first sc to join.

BASIC MESH PATTERN

Rnd 1: Ch 5 (counts as dc, ch 2), sk next 2 sts, (dc in next st, ch 2, skip next 2 sts) around until 3 sts rem, dc in next st, hdc in 3rd ch of beg ch-5 to join – 12 squares.

The joining hdc creates the last sp of the rnd and sets you up in the correct position to begin the next rnd in the center of the last sp.

Rnd 2: Ch 5 (counts as dc, ch 2), (dc in next ch-2 sp, ch 2) around until 1 sp rem, dc in last ch-2 sp, hdc in 3rd ch of beg ch-5 to join.

Rep Rnd 2 until desired height.

Last rnd: Ch 1, 2 sc in sp created by joining hdc, work 3 dc in each ch-2 sp around to end, sc in same sp as the first sc, sl st in first sc to join.

Fasten off and weave in any loose ends. Follow Finishing instructions to stiffen fiber.

JUTE

Materials

50 yards (46 m) lightweight jute twine in brown

Size 5.0 mm (H/8) hook

Instructions

Work Closed Base as for Kitchen String vase through Rnd 5.

Next rnd: Ch 1, sc in blo of each st around, sl st in first sc to join.

Continue to work sc through both loops for 3 rnds.

STACKED MESH PATTERN

Rnd 1: Ch 5 (counts as dc, ch 2), sk next 2 sts, *dc in each of next 4 sts, ch 2, sk next 2 sts, dc in next st, ch 2, skip next 2 sts; rep from * around, sl st in 3rd ch of beg ch-5 to join.

This is a basic square pattern; replace an occasional ch-2 with 2 dc in each of next 2 ch sts to form random blocks of dc sts.

Rnd 2: Ch 5 (counts as dc, ch 2), (dc in next dc, ch 2) around, sl st in 3rd ch of beg ch-5 to join.

Rep Rnd 2 until desired height.

Last rnd: Ch 1, sc in same st as sl st, sc evenly around working 1 sc in each st and 2 sc in each ch-2 sp, sl st in first sc to join.

Fasten off and weave in any loose ends. Follow Finishing instructions to stiffen fiber.

Finishing (for all three projects)

Using 3 parts fabric stiffener (glue) to 1 part water, pour enough glue mixture to cover the bottom of a plastic bag. Place the cylinder in the bag and squish to cover the surface with the solution. Remove the cylinder and pat with a paper towel to remove excess glue. Bend a piece of plastic mesh into a tube to make the form, or use a glass big enough to help the cylinder keep its shape while it dries. Insert the form, smooth the piece to the desired shape, and set in a warm place to dry completely. It should only take a couple of hours to set.

Variations

You can stitch up the bases with almost any fiber, including jute, twine, and cotton thread.

Make the vases larger or smaller by adding or removing rounds of increases to change the width and adjusting the rows to change the height.

Experiment with the mesh patterns, using taller stitches and additional chain stitches to create larger spaces.

martini Bag

Recently, I became obsessed with felted beads. Because they are so much fun to make, I forced every kid I knew to make them with me. My daughter and I made lots of them, big and small. We experimented with layers of color so that when we cut the curved ends of the ball we could make round, flat felted beads with multiple rings of color. I created this little bag specifically so I could use felted beads in the strap. This particular combination of colors reminds me of green olives and pimentos, which can only lead to a martini from there.

Finished Size

Before felting: 8 1/2" (w) x 8 3/4" (h) x 1 1/4" (d) [21.5 cm x 22 cm x 3 cm]

After felting: 6" (w) x 7" (h) x 1" (d) [15 cm x 18 cm x 2.5 cm], not including strap

Materials

BAG

Cascade 220 (100% Peruvian highland wool; 220 yds [201 m]; 3.5 ounces [100 g]; CYCA #4 Worsted)

    1 skein #9465 pimento (MC)
    1 skein #2409 olive (CC)

Size 5.5 mm (I/9) hook

Yarn needle

Pins

1 yard (1 m) scrap cotton yarn or thread

Scrap yarn in dark orange, for embroidering button hole (optional)

FELTED BEADS

1/2 ounce orange roving

1/2 ounce dark green roving

1/2 ounce light green roving

15 to 20 Darice green glass beads mix #1972-90

30 inches (76 cm) Beadalon bead stringing wire (.46 mm, 20 lb) in green

2 gold crimp beads

2 Blue Moon Beads gold metal clasp hooks or any heavyweight clasp hooks

Needle-nose pliers

Gauge

14 hdc-flo x 9 rows = 4" (10 cm) using MC

Design Notes

- Roving is what loose animal fibers look like before being spun into yarn. Spinning supply shops carry dyed and natural roving in large rolls or small packages. Since felting has become popular, many yarn and craft shops also carry small quantities of roving in their yarn sections. Just 1/2 ounce of roving will make several beads.

- The body of the bag is made in three separate pieces. The front and back panels are joined together with a long piece that forms the gusset.

- The strap is made with beading wire and a variety of felted and glass beads.

- The turning chain does not count as a stitch unless otherwise instructed.

Stitch Guide

Hdc-flo: Half double crochet through the front loop of the stitch.

French knot: Bring the needle up through the fabric to the RS. Holding the needle 2 inches (5 cm) away from the button, pinch the yarn 1 inch (2.5 cm) from the fabric with your left thumb and index finger. Bring the needle to the section of yarn below your thumb. With the point of the needle facing up, loop the yarn with your left hand around the needle three times. Still pinching the yarn with your left hand and pulling tight to keep the loops from falling off, rotate the needle so it points down and push it through the fabric close to where you originally started.

Instructions

FRONT

With MC, ch 9.

Row 1: Hdc in 2nd ch from hook and in each ch across, turn – 8 hdc.

Row 2: Ch 3, hdc in 2nd ch from hook, hdc in next ch, hdc-flo in each st across, [hdc into the vertical threads on the side of the last st (see page 37)] twice, turn – 12 hdc.

Rows 3–4: Rep Row 2 ending with 20 hdc.

Row 5: Ch 1, 2 hdc-flo in the first st, hdc-flo in each st across to last st, 2 hdc-flo in last st, turn – 22 hdc.

Rows 6–7: Rep Row 5 ending with 26 hdc.

Row 8: Ch 1, hdc-flo in each st across, turn.

Row 9: Rep Row 5 – 28 hdc.

Rows 10–11: Rep Rows 8 and 9 ending with 30 hdc.

Rows 12–20: Rep Row 8.

Fasten off and loosely weave in ends with a yarn needle.

BACK

Work as for front but do not fasten off. Continue on to flap.

FLAP

Rows 1–5: Ch 1, hdc-flo in each st across, turn.

Row 6: Do not ch 1, skip first st, hdc-flo in each st across to last st, turn leaving rem st unworked – 28 sts.

Repeat Row 6, decreasing each row by 2 sts, until there are only 10 sts remaining.

Fasten off and loosely weave in ends.

GUSSET

With CC, ch 6.

Row 1: Hdc in 2nd ch from hook and in each ch across, turn – 5 hdc.

Row 2: Ch 1, hdc-flo in each st across, turn.

Rep Row 2 until gusset measures about 24 inches (61 cm).

Fasten off and loosely weave in ends.

Finishing

With WS together, pin the gusset to the front panel leaving 2 inches (5 cm) of gusset extending from each side of the top edge for the strap tabs. Join MC and sc gusset and front together. Repeat for back, leaving flap unattached.

Fold tabs down 1 inch (2.5 cm) to WS and sew to gusset, creating a pocket for the clasp hook after felting.

With yarn needle and cotton yarn or thread, baste the opening of the front and back together. Baste the flap to the front panel of the bag.

Follow the instructions on page 44 for felting in the washing machine. Once the bag has felted to size, roll it in a towel to remove any excess water. Remove the cotton basting thread and shape the flap as shown. If the flap is a little wonky, trim it with a pair of sharp scissors. Give any rough edges a quick felt by hand using hot, soapy water. Stuff the bag with plastic grocery bags to form the shape, pin the flap to the bag, and set it in a warm place to dry completely.

FELTED BEADS FOR STRAP (Make 10 of varying sizes from 1/2 to 1 1/2 inches [1 to 4 cm] in diameter, plus one bead 1/2 inch [1 cm] in diameter for the button)

Prepare a bowl of hot water with a squirt of detergent or 2 tablespoons of baking soda. Take a strand of roving about 16 inches (40.5 cm) long and 1 inch (2.5 cm) wide. Spread and

fluff the fibers a little to loosen. Begin rolling the wool into a ball, wrapping the loose roving around your fingers as you would wind a ball of yarn (see photo at left), until it is roughly twice as big as you want it to be after felting. Dip the ball into the water to get it thoroughly wet. Pat the ball with your fingers to encourage the fibers to latch onto each other. As the fibers begin to mat and intertwine, gently roll the ball between your hands. As the ball starts to shrink you can roll it more quickly and firmly. If you need to add more fiber, simply take additional roving, fan out the fibers, and wrap them around the ball, then dip the ball in water and roll it between your hands. Repeat the wrap, dip, and roll until the ball is about the size you want it to be. Dip it in cold water to remove any excess detergent, roll it in a towel to remove any excess water, and set it in a warm place to dry completely.

To make the bead hole, push a knitting needle, skewer, or toothpick all the way through the center of the bead.

BUTTON HOLE

Poke a knitting needle or other pointy object through the bag flap 1 1/2 to 2 inches (4 to 5 cm) from the bottom edge. Trim around the hole to widen it until the small felted bead can push through. Use the orange yarn and a yarn needle to embroider or stitch around the hole with a blanket stitch (see page 65). Pull a small piece of yarn through the button and make a French knot (see page 153). Using the button hole as a guide, push the tail ends from the French knot through the front panel and make a couple of small sts in the same spot to secure the button.

STRINGING THE BEADS

Lay out the felted and glass beads for the strap and reposition until you like the pattern. Begin to string the beads onto the wire, adding a crimp bead after the first 2 or 3 beads and before the last 2 or 3 beads (do not crimp yet). Draw out another 5 inches (13 cm) of beading wire and cut. Thread one end of the beading wire through the small ring of one hook closure, then thread the wire back through the first couple of

FELT BEAD TIPS:

- Be gentle with the beads at first until the fibers begin to adhere to each other.
- Try to keep the inside of the bead a little loose and lofty to make it easier to poke a hole through. To do this, keep the first layer of roving pretty loose. As you add layers of roving, felt the additional layers more tightly by rubbing the bead more vigorously.
- If the bead isn't the right size, add more layers of loose roving and continue felting.
- If the bead won't stick together in some places, trim it with scissors, then add more layers of loose roving.

beads and the crimping bead. Pushing the crimping bead snug against the bead below it, crimp the bead with needle-nose pliers to secure the wire end. Repeat for the second end of the beading wire, pulling the wire tight to make sure there isn't a lot of excess wire between beads. Snip any extra wire. Attach the hook closures to the gusset tabs on the bag. If the pocket of a tab happened to felt shut, just poke a knitting needle or pen through to loosen it up.

Variations

Add chain stitches to the gusset to make it wider. The wider the gusset, the deeper the bag.

Use all glass beads to create the strap.

Cut the felted beads in half to make half-moon beads or cut the rounded end off opposing sides to make a flat bead.

Loosely layer additional colors of roving around the bead to give it a mottled effect.

ABBREVIATIONS AND SYMBOLS

Here are a few common abbreviations and terms found in crochet patterns.

approx	approximately
beg	beginning
bet	between
blo	back loop only
CC	contrasting color
ch	chain stitch
ch-	refers to chain or space previously made: e.g., ch-1 space
ch sp	chain space
cm	centimeter
cont	continue
dc	double crochet
dc2tog	double crochet 2 stitches together
dec	decrease
dtr	double treble
e	extended (i.e., esc)
fdc	foundation double crochet
fhdc	foundation half double crochet

flo	front loop only
foll	following
fsc	foundation single crochet
g	grams
hdc	half double crochet
inc	increase
m	meters
MC	main color
mm	millimeters
oz	ounce(s)
patt	pattern
prev	previous
rem	remain/remaining
rep	repeat(s)
rev sc	reverse single crochet
rnd(s)	round(s)
RS	right side
sc	single crochet

sc2tog	single crochet 2 stitches together
sk	skip
sl st	slip stitch
sp(s)	space(s)
st(s)	stitch(es)
tch	turning chain
tog	together
tr	treble
WS	wrong side
yd(s)	yard(s)
yo	yarn over
*	repeat the instructions following the asterisk as directed
( ) and [ ]	repeat the instructions in parentheses or brackets the number of times as directed
** ... **	repeat the pattern instructions from ** to **

RESOURCES

BAG-MAKING SUPPLIES

M&J Trimming • www.mjtrim.com • 800-9-MJTRIM

Trims, tassels, handbag handles, buttons, rhinestones, cords, and nailheads. M&J Trimming has everything you need when it comes to unique trims and embellishments.

Tall Poppy Craft Products • www.tallpoppycraft.com • 212-813-3223

Tall Poppy Craft has a unique assortment of bag-making supplies, including beautiful handles, hardware, and fabrics.

UMX Fashion Supplies • www.umei.com • 800-921-5523

UMX is an online factory-direct fashion supply store with an amazing selection of bag-making accessories, including handles and straps in a wide variety of colors and sizes.

CRAFTING COMMUNITIES

Craftster • www.craftster.org

If your craft involves yarn, glue, glitter, thread, nails, needles, or really anything at all—there is a place for you on Craftster. It offers discussion boards, tutorials, and contests to challenge your creativity.

Crochet me • www.crochetme.com

Crochet Me started as an online magazine dedicated to providing free contemporary crochet patterns, articles, and how-tos. It has since evolved into a community for sharing projects, tips, and patterns.

Crochetville • www.crochetville.org

Crochetville is one of the first online communities dedicated solely to crochet, including patterns, tutorials, websites, and design.

Ravelry • www.ravelry.com

Ravelry is a super fun community for people interested in crochet, knitting, spinning, and other fiber arts. Use the site to organize and manage your yarn and projects, or connect with others who have similar interests in photo sharing groups and forums.

EDUCATIONAL RESOURCES

Art of Crochet.com • www.artofcrochet.com

A complement to any crochet book, this website features an online library of video stitch guides for basic to advanced stitchers and righties as well as lefties.

Crochet Guild of America • http://crochet.org

The CGOA is a nonprofit educational organization dedicated to preserving and passing on the fine art of crochet.

Yarnstandards.com • www.yarnstandards.com

An online resource of yarn and design information compiled by the Craft Yarn Council of America with the cooperation of industry publishers, designers, and manufacturers. You'll find standard crochet abbreviations and hook sizes along with the standard sizes for body measurements to be used in designing garments.

FABRIC

Amy Butler • www.amybutlerdesign.com • 740-587-2841

Amy Butler creates gorgeous fabrics with artistic style.

Moda Fabrics • www.unitednotions.com • 800-527-9447

Moda produces beautiful fabrics to match any style.

Reprodepot • www.reprodepot.com • 877-RETROFAB

If you love vintage fabric, you'll love Reprodepot. They carry a wide selection of fabrics that are either directly reproduced from vintage designs or just inspired by them. They also carry ribbon and trim.

FIBER

Berroco • www.berroco.com • 508-278-2527

Berroco has a vast selection of traditional and novelty yarns that are usually available in most yarn shops.

FIBER, continued

Brown Sheep Company • www.brownsheep.com • 800-826-9136

Brown Sheep produces my favorite wool brand, Lamb's Pride. The yarns are soft and wonderful to work with and your felted projects will shrink quickly and beautifully.

Cascade Yarns • www.cascadeyarns.com

Cascade's 220 wools always felt nicely and the Pastaza wools have a soft, delicate fuzziness after felting due to the 50 percent llama wool content.

Darice • www.darice.com • 800-321-1494

Darice is one of the largest distributers of craft supplies. Their products include beads, wire, and hemp that are usually available at craft supply chain stores like JoAnn Fabrics and Michaels.

Hemp Basics, LLC • www.hempbasics.com • 888-831-3747

Hemp Basics manufactures and distributes hemp twine, cord, and fabrics. Includes polished, unpolished, bleached, semi-bleached, non-bleached, and dyed hemp cord and twine in several plies and weights.

Home Depot • www.homedepot.com • 800-553-3199

I buy almost all of my kitchen string, jute, and sisal supplies at Home Depot. They also carry grommets and grommet-setting tools.

Jewelry Supply.com • www.jewelrysupply.com • 866-380-7464

Jewelry Supply.com is an online jewelry-making supply store that also happens to carry leather cord in a variety of colors and lengths. You can usually get a discount if you buy multiple spools.

Knitpicks • www.knitpicks.com • 800-574-1323

Knitpicks has a large selection of mostly wool fibers for a steal.

Kpixie • www.kpixie.com • 508-378-7344

Kpixie is right on top of current trends in fibers. Their inventory is an eclectic mix of specialty yarns and fibers, including wool, cotton, handspun, import, and paper fibers.

Land of Odds • www.landofodds.com • 615-292-0610

Land of Odds is an excellent resource for inexpensive beads and jewelry-making supplies. This is also a great place to shop for wire.

Leather Cord Online • www.leathercordonline.com • 937-399-4645

This is where I get most of my leather cord. They sell imported leather in 25-yard (23 m) spools in a wide range of sizes and colors. The owner ships quickly and offers discounts for multiple quantities.

Lily • www.sugarncream.com • 888-368-8401

Lily is known for its Sugar 'n Cream yarns—good-value cotton yarns available almost anywhere in a wide range of colors.

Paper Mart • www.papermart.com • 800-745-8800

Papermart carries a wide selection of packaging supplies, including ribbons, cording, raffia, jute twine, cotton string, and many elastic and nonelastic cords.

Weaving Works • www.weavingworks.com • 888-524-1221

Weaving Works is my favorite store in the Seattle area. They have a beautiful selection of yarns and spinning supplies, including dyed and natural roving, and the people are so friendly. If you're lucky enough to live close by, be sure to arrive when tea is being served.

NOTIONS AND ACCESSORIES

Create for Less • www.createforless.com • 866-333-4463

Create for Less is a beautiful thing. They have more than 50,000 craft supplies and everything is discounted. They sell crochet, embroidery, and felting tools and accessories, including hooks, roving, embroidery floss, and yarn.

Crippenworks • www.crippenworks.com • 518-789-6703

Katharyn Crippen Shapiro creates beautiful custom-made needle and hook cases. When you visit her website, you choose the fabric for your case. If you need extra pockets or any other adjustments, she is happy to customize to your specifications.

DMC Corporation • www.dmc-usa.com • 973-589-0606

DMC has the one of the largest selections of needlework threads on the planet.

Fire Mountain Gems • www.firemountaingems.com • 800-355-2137

One of the few places that sells Chinese coin replicas in a variety of sizes along with beads and other jewelry-making supplies.

The Warm Company • www.warmcompany.com • 425-248-2424

These are the fine makers of Steam-a-Seam fusible web products.

INDEX